ROUTLEDGE LIBRARY EDITIONS: LIBRARY AND INFORMATION SCIENCE

Volume 81

ROLE OF TECHNICAL REPORTS IN SCI-TECH LIBRARIES

ROLE OF TECHNICAL REPORTS IN SCI-TECH LIBRARIES

Edited by
ELLIS MOUNT

LONDON AND NEW YORK

First published in 1982 by The Haworth Press, Inc.

This edition first published in 2020
by Routledge
2 Park Square, Milton Park, Abingdon, Oxon OX14 4RN

and by Routledge
52 Vanderbilt Avenue, New York, NY 10017

Routledge is an imprint of the Taylor & Francis Group, an informa business

© 1982 The Haworth Press, Inc.

All rights reserved. No part of this book may be reprinted or reproduced or utilised in any form or by any electronic, mechanical, or other means, now known or hereafter invented, including photocopying and recording, or in any information storage or retrieval system, without permission in writing from the publishers.

Trademark notice: Product or corporate names may be trademarks or registered trademarks, and are used only for identification and explanation without intent to infringe.

British Library Cataloguing in Publication Data
A catalogue record for this book is available from the British Library

ISBN: 978-0-367-34616-4 (Set)
ISBN: 978-0-429-34352-0 (Set) (ebk)
ISBN: 978-0-367-41874-8 (Volume 81) (hbk)
ISBN: 978-0-367-41875-5 (Volume 81) (pbk)
ISBN: 978-0-367-81672-8 (Volume 81) (ebk)

Publisher's Note
The publisher has gone to great lengths to ensure the quality of this reprint but points out that some imperfections in the original copies may be apparent.

Disclaimer
The publisher has made every effort to trace copyright holders and would welcome correspondence from those they have been unable to trace.

Role of Technical Reports in Sci-Tech Libraries

Ellis Mount, Editor

Volume 1, Number 4, Summer 1981
Science & Technology Libraries

The Haworth Press
New York

Science & Technology Libraries is published quarterly in Fall, Winter, Spring, and Summer.

MANUSCRIPTS should be submitted in triplicate to Ellis Mount, DLS, School of Library Service, Columbia University, Butler Library, New York, NY 10027. All editorial inquiries should be directed to the Editor. Refer to the Instructions for Authors page (at the end of this issue) for additional manuscript submission requirements.

BUSINESS OFFICE. All subscription and advertising inquiries should be directed to The Haworth Press, 28 East 22 Street, New York, NY 10010.

SUBSCRIPTIONS are on an academic year, per volume basis only. Payment must be made in U.S. or Canadian funds only. $42.00. Postage and handling: U.S. orders, add $1.75; Canadian orders, add $6.00 U.S. currency or $6.50 Canadian currency. Foreign orders: individuals, add $20.00; institutions, add $30.00; libraries, add $40.00 (includes postage and handling).

CHANGE OF ADDRESS. Please notify the Subscription Department, The Haworth Press, 75 Griswold Street, Binghamton, NY 13904 of address changes. Please allow six weeks for processing; include old and new addresses, including both zip codes.

Copyright © 1982 by The Haworth Press, Inc. All rights reserved. Copies of articles in this journal may be reproduced noncommercially for the purpose of educational or scientific advancement. Otherwise, no part of this work may be reproduced or utilized in any form or by any means, electronic or mechanical, including photocopying, microfilm, and recording, or by any information storage and retrieval system, without permission in writing from the publisher. Printed in the United States of America.

Application to mail at second-class postal rates pending at New York, NY and additional mailing offices.

POSTMASTER: Send address changes to The Haworth Press, 28 East 22 Street, New York, NY 10010.

Library of Congress Cataloging in Publication Data
Main entry under title:

Role of technical reports in sci-tech libraries.

 (Science & technology libraries ; v. 1, no. 4)
 Includes bibliographical references.
 1. Scientific libraries—United States. 2. Technical libraries—United States. 3. Technical reports. I. Mount, Ellis. II. Series: Science and technology libraries ; v. 1, no. 4.
Z675.T3R56   026.5   81-7231
ISBN 0-917724-74-7 (pbk.)   AACR2

Science & Technology Libraries

THEME OF THIS ISSUE
Role of Technical Reports in Sci-Tech Libraries

Volume 1
Number 4
Summer 1981

EDITORIAL	1
INTRODUCTION: Role of Technical Reports in Sci-Tech Libraries *Irving M. Klempner*	3
Interaction Within the Technical Reports Community *Ruth S. Smith*	5
Some Aspects of Technical Report Processing by Federal Agencies *Madeline M. Henderson*	19
Managing the Bell Laboratories Technical Report Service *Amy Wang* *Diane M. Alimena*	27
Three Technical Report Printed Indexes: A Comparative Study *Susan Copeland*	41
Managing Exxon's Technical Reports *Karen Landsberg* *Ben H. Weil*	55

Laboratory Notebook Storage and Retrieval Systems 65
 C. Margaret Bell

NEW REFERENCE WORKS IN SCIENCE & TECHNOLOGY 73
 Janice W. Bain, Editor

SCI-TECH ONLINE 77
 Ellen Nagle, Editor

EDITORIAL

One of the distinguishing characteristics of sci-tech libraries is the different types of materials they collect as compared to other kinds of libraries. This issue focuses attention on one important source of sci-tech information, the technical report. An introduction to the issue has been prepared by Irving M. Klempner, who is a member of the faculty of the School of Library and Information Science at the State University of New York at Albany. Dr. Klempner has written extensively on the nature and use of technical reports and is thus well qualified to comment on this particular topic.

Our special paper in this issue is on a type of material that is also important to many sci-tech libraries, namely laboratory notebooks. The article was written by C. Margaret Bell, an employee at the information center of General Foods in Tarrytown, New York. The paucity of information published on this topic makes this contributed paper doubly welcome.

Ellis Mount

INTRODUCTION: ROLE OF TECHNICAL REPORTS IN SCI-TECH LIBRARIES

The literature of technical reports clearly constitutes a vital source of information for almost all areas of science and technology. An increasing number of industrial organizations and private institutions have been engaged in carrying out research and development activities and have been the major producers of the technical reports literature. During the past decade alone, more than $400 billion has been expended in the United States on research and development (R&D). The product of this expenditure has been, for the most part, recorded information in the form of the technical report.

Federal R&D obligations for fiscal years 1981 and 1982 are estimated to be $35.2 and $41.7 billion respectively, and, as in the past, the major portion of the work is to be performed under contract or grant by the private sector of our economy. Historically, more than half of all of the U.S. funding for R&D has been provided by the Federal government. Federal government agencies, state, county and municipal governments, regional authorities, foreign governments, their laboratories and information centers also produce many thousands of technical reports.

While an ever-widening spectrum of subject matter is being embraced by the literature of technical reports, it has also become clear that neat compartmentalization of science and technology is neither possible nor desirable. Increasingly, science and technology have become intertwined with regulatory, environmental or socio-political factors that often exert a controlling influence not only on the development and application of scientific and technological innovations, but also on their underlying research orientations.

It has been documented that in our post-industrial economy, an estimated 45 percent of the Gross National Product and 58 percent of our work force is engaged in some form of information-handling activity. Librarians and information specialists familiar with the literature of technical reports could readily perceive the vital role for that literature in solving many of our technical and societal problems. Yet, as is evidenced in Madeline Henderson's contribution to this issue of *Science & Technology Libraries*, compared to the monographic literature, the literature of technical reports has been given scant professional attention or adequate public recognition. Forgotten collections of technical reports are to be found in the Smithsonian Institution, the Library of Congress or at Texas A & M University's Center for Energy and Mineral Resources where minimal efforts are currently underway to translate and organize 500,000 pages of documents on the synthetic fuels industry, seized by allied forces in Germany in 1945. Moreover, even the latest edition of the *Anglo-American Cataloguing Rules* contains no references to such bibliographic elements as contract number, sponsoring agency, sub-contractor, etc. The term "technical report" or "research report" is not to be found in the AACR 2 index. Although more than 100,000 technical reports are produced annually in the United States, and although close to 200 Federal information clearinghouses have functions with respect to organization and servicing of federally funded information resources, no one organization has been given the responsibility to coordinate the processing and dissemination of the technical reports literature. Perhaps what we are dealing with here is not malevolent conspiracy but rather a form of benign neglect. Ruth Smith's contribution reinforces the Henderson thesis of the value of reports and the desirability of interaction, cooperative sharing and networking not only within the Federal government, but also with information handling facilities in the private sectors of our economy.

It would follow that whenever national attention is not focused on the organization of a particular literature, individual libraries would be forced to expend their own resources in developing internal systems for the control and servicing of that literature. Of course, unique local information needs, production of internal or limited distribution reports, the desirability of implementing customized current awareness services or specialized indexing and abstracting procedures and similar measures would call for the development of sometimes unique and local procedures.

Amy Wang and Diane M. Alimena deal in considerable detail with the reports collections maintained by Bell Laboratories as well as their indexing and current awareness services designed for maximum utilization. The contribution dealing with the management of Exxon's reports literature provides yet another example of customized services for the literature of technical reports, as described by Karen Landsberg and Ben H. Weil.

Susan Copeland's comparative study and analysis of the abstracting and indexing services of NASA's *Scientific and Technical Aerospace Reports*, DOE's *Energy Research Abstracts* and NTIS's *Government Reports Announcements & Index* focuses on areas of duplication, indexing variations, structure and coverage for these printed indexes.

It is, I believe, beyond dispute that the literature of technical reports will continue to play a vital role as a medium for the communication of research results. The issue of this journal specifically devoted to the analysis of problems, innovative practices and advances relating to the control and servicing of that literature will undoubtedly be of benefit not only to science and technology librarians, but to the profession at large.

Irving M. Klempner
School of Library and Information Science
State University of New York at Albany

INTERACTION WITHIN THE TECHNICAL REPORTS COMMUNITY

Ruth S. Smith

ABSTRACT. There is a growing interdependence among the major Federal technical reports processing agencies, the science/technology libraries/information centers and commercial services with which they interact. In this interconnected information network, the participants both feed and use the system to fulfill their missions in regard to transferring government research and development results. Cooperative arrangements between and among the participants and a sharing of resources are becoming increasingly imperative in order to lower costs and increase efficiency. Recent steps taken toward updating standards, sharing resources and moving toward closer cooperation are described.

For many years, the value of technical reports has been obscured by their lack of glamour and the bibliographic problems they create for catalogers. They have several unique features, such as a report number, a contract number, a sponsoring agency as well as an originating agency, and often are written by a study team rather than a single author. They can be interim reports, progress reports, or final reports. They can be proposals, testimony before Congress or the proceedings of a conference. Their formats vary. They might be brief (two pages) or lengthy (500 pages). They appear as microfiche, computer printouts or vu-graphs, and often they are looseleaf (with periodic changes that need to be inserted) or have a paper cover, and often contain foldouts. They slump on the shelf, their staples or prong fasteners snag other documents on the shelf, and they are just not neat.

Once the orphans of legitimate literature because they were considered "unpublished" literature, technical reports recently have taken on an increasing respectability due to their value to research and development scientists and engineers. This literature is often the only source of information about current and/or projected research. Therefore, they are vital to most government and government-contractor scientific and technical libraries/information centers. They also are bread and butter staples of the government information services which serve the R&D community.

The Federal A&I Community

In order to maintain technological leadership, there was an increased urgency in this country to push ahead with scientific and technical research and development after the launching of the first space satellite

Ruth S. Smith is Manager, Technical Information Services, Institute for Defense Analyses, 400 Army Navy Drive, Arlington, VA 22202. She holds an AB from Wayne State University and an ABLS from the University of Michigan.

by the Russians. New concepts and developments often were discussed in report literature long before anything appeared in print in technical journals or books (if it ever did). The demand for technical reports was great among R&D scientists. Distribution often was informally achieved by the scientists and engineers themselves, from colleague to colleague working in the same field. When a researcher would hear about a report at a conference, quite often he would ask the library to track it down with only bits of information—a report number, a source, part of a title, date, or general topic. The search for this elusive material was challenging, indeed. Libraries maintained locator information and card files, which were kept long after the documents were gone, because there were no adequate printed indexes available.

Agencies

The agencies sponsoring the research as well as the contracting companies or grantees were faced with an ever growing problem of controlling the R&D work being done as well as the ever mounting volume of reports literature being produced. Rapid access to this information was a priority. R&D was urgent, so it should not be delayed. There was little need to repeat work if it already had been done.

Federal document centers were established to abstract, index, and distribute government sponsored or produced scientific and technical reports. The four major successors to those early documentation centers are: the National Aeronautics and Space Administration's Scientific and Technical Information Facility (NASA/STIF), the National Technical Information Service (NTIS), the Defense Technical Information Center (DTIC), and the Department of Energy's Technical Information Center (DOE/TIC). These agencies were the core of the Federal abstracting and indexing (A&I) community. Other agencies with similar interests had libraries and centers, too. The literature is replete with accounts of the early struggles of their predecessors, the problems and the frustrations of controlling the "information explosion." They have come a long way since then.

Libraries/Information Centers

The libraries and information centers which provided the scientists with information were faced with similar problems—the volume of material, its elusive nature and the pressing need to identify and obtain it as quickly as possible. The volume of technical reports to process was prodigious and their shelf life was relatively short. Standard library cataloging was detailed and slow. It also was expensive. Reports were difficult to catalog because they followed no standard pattern. The clues needed for user-oriented retrieval might be any level of a corporate author's name, contracting agency, contract number, report number (often more than one) and key word descriptors. The latter were especially important to capture newly emerging concepts and catch-word identifiers. Many libraries developed home-grown short-cuts for cataloging this unique body of literature. Quite often the short-cuts used at the input stage have made the systems awkward and difficult to use for retrieval purposes. So, as the Government information services improved, libraries were inclined to rely more heavily on the abstracting, indexing and announcement of the major A&I agencies. Many patterned their own card catalogs after the indexing of the agency they used the most.

The Private Sector

The private sector is a participant in this community, too. Contractors often supply documents, bibliographic records or processing services for the government.
The Department of Energy Technical Information Center (DOE/TIC) at Oak Ridge (TN) has a contractor on-site who sells microfiche and printed copies of DOE reports to DOE organizations, contractors, universities and other government agencies; the National Technical Information Service makes these reports available to the public. DOE's Energy Data Base and others, such as the NTIS bibliographic file, are searchable online through the commercial online data base services.
The NASA Scientific and Technical Information Facility (NASA/STIF) at Baltimore-Washington Airport (MD), under contract to the NASA Scientific and Technical Information Office (NASA/STIO), collects, accessions, indexes, announces and distributes reports issued by, or of interest to, the aerospace community. Also under contract to NASA/STIO, the American Institute of Aeronautics and Astronautics (AIAA) provides abstracting and indexing services covering the world's published literature and "unpublished" reports in the fields of aeronautics and space science and technology; the abstracts and indexes for the reports literature (unpublished) are input to the NASA/STIF for publication in *Scientific and Technical Aerospace Reports* (STAR), while the open literature (published) is announced by AIAA in *International Aerospace Abstracts*. The European Space Agency in Paris has a special information exchange agreement with NASA/STIO to acquire and descriptively catalog documents for the central computerized file at NASA/STIF.

Interdependence

This community is an interconnected information network. Agencies produce reports, have contractors and grantees who produce reports, and thus feed the system. Through interagency agreements and contracts with the private sector, information is transferred to support the mission of each of the participants as well as the overall R&D effort.
Each agency, for example, has a mission to perform. Each maintains an information system which collects, indexes and abstracts, announces and distributes reports to fulfill this mission. However, these agencies have overlapping interests in scientific and technological R&D and exchange bibliographic tapes and, sometimes, copies of documents. The

tapes received from others are screened for relevant information and the entries are adapted so they can be merged with the agency's own data base. The purpose is to better serve the agency's own specific mission.

DOE, DTIC and NASA all send tapes and microfiche copies of reports to NTIS, which acts as the centralized outlet for the sale to the general public. NTIS also maintains deposit accounts and handles the collection of payments for documents supplied by DTIC to its own user community.

Moves Toward Standardization

Over the years there have been moves toward greater standardization between and among the participants in this technical reports community. Some prime examples are the updating of the COSATI standards and work toward development of a coordinated data element dictionary.

COSATI Background

In the early 60's, in order to provide consistency among the agencies engaged in abstracting and indexing technical reports, the Committee on Scientific and Technical Information (COSATI) was formed under the wing of the Federal Council for Science and Technology. The COSATI participants were representatives from the major technical reports handling agencies. Together they developed the *COSATI Standard for Descriptive Cataloging of Government Scientific and Technical Reports*.[1]

When COSATI was transferred to the National Science Foundation in 1966, its funding dwindled and it was allowed to die. This left no coordinated mechanism for keeping the rules up to date. So, when minor revisions or new rules were needed, the agencies made decisions on their own or with other agencies, which created some variations in applications of the standard.

Need for Updating COSATI

In 1977, there was a rebirth of interest in updating the COSATI rules. Initiatives came from within the technical reports community itself—from the technology-based information agencies who needed to lower costs and improve the efficiency of their systems, and from representatives of scientific and technical libraries and information centers who wanted to improve speed of access to government R&D information.

Hubert E. Sauter, Administrator of the Defense Documentation Center (now the Defense Technical Information Center) assembled a small group at DDC in April of 1977 to discuss use of the COSATI standard for descriptive cataloging of technical reports. The nine people present represented DDC, the Environmental Protection Agency (EPA), the National Aeronautics and Space Administration (NASA), the Energy Research and Development Administration (ERDA) (now the Department of Energy), the National Technical Information Service (NTIS), the National Oceanic and Atmospheric Administration (NOAA), and the Institute for Defense Analyses (IDA). They concluded that (a) the span of the Federal A&I community's interests included report literature, in toto, and not just scientific and technical reports, (b) a communications device is needed that will allow users to draw out what each wants from the cataloging record, and (c) this requires thinking in terms of online use of records and communications formats. A coordinated approach to mutual problems was deemed desirable. The group determined to meet again soon.

In July and December of that same year, the Committee on Information Hang-ups held meetings which were related to this DDC initiative. (The Committee, founded and coordinated by the author, is an informal group of librarians and information specialists from government and non-government libraries/information centers in the Washington area whose sole purpose is to identify information problems, establish communication between users and producers of government information and try to improve the overall system; it has established a dialogue with the major government information processors over the past eleven years and these activities have been successful in bringing about some of the improvements recommended by the librarians/information specialists.) At the July meeting of the Committee, Sarah Kadec, then Chief of the Library Systems Branch, Management and Organization Division, Environmental Protection Agency, spoke on "The Decision to Use the COSATI format in EPA" to establish a single bibliographic file from four of its existing specialized files. Their requirements were as follows: a single contractor; a single thesaurus; a single file and bibliographic format; an ability to build on existing files; and a single format for all types of materials. Ten reasons for choosing the COSATI Format were cited. In these, the overriding consideration was the user—defined as anyone and everyone (not necessarily librarians). The EPA file is basically a retrieval tool and not a catalog of holdings. Cataloging is done from the publication (names which change are cross referenced in the file). A feature of the COSATI system is its ability to accept change and updating. However, she pointed out there has been no official updating of COSATI since 1966 and at present there is no formal mechanism for updating it. "We have met recently with others who are concerned with this problem," she said, "and are hopeful that some formal mechanism can be developed."

After the meeting, Kadec wrote to the Chairman of the Committee on Information Hang-ups, "Your group seems a likely one to develop further our idea of a task force to keep the COSATI standard up to date. Individual agencies could then report missing elements or desired changes to this task force for review and action."

In September that same year, Sauter spoke to the Committee on Information Hang-ups on "Standard Descriptive Cataloging of Government Scientific and Technical Reports." He said the purpose of the COSATI standard was to bring the descriptive cataloging practices of the major technical report producing agencies closer together, and this was achieved before the COSATI Sub Panel on Descriptive Cataloging stopped functioning (with COSATI's demise). Agencies did make changes and often worked with other agencies to make joint changes. DDC continued to use the COSATI standard for two reasons in addition to those outlined by Kadec: (a) it appears to be considerably less expensive to apply than the Anglo-American Cataloging Rules (AACR), and (b) there are more than 1,200,000 records at present in DDC files. He suggested a number of ways in which the COSATI standard could be updated, but concluded that "an unbiased, but interested third party" should take on the task. He proposed that the Committee on Information Hang-ups establish a working group to study the COSATI descriptive cataloging standard to determine who uses it, the pros and cons of using it, the problems there are with its use and ways of revising and keeping it up to date. "The working group should, of course, have representation from the agencies that participated in the original effort as well as other interested agencies, and most important, the user community." The Committee accepted the challenge to study at least the first part of the problem: Determine the use of the standard and the reasons for using it. The possible follow-on would be to look at the problems of using it and ways of strengthening the system from within, so it could move toward consistent interaction with other networks in the future.

Working Group on Updating COSATI

In November 1977, the Committee on Information Hang-ups called a meeting of representatives of the original agencies which produced the COSATI guidelines and interested librarians and information specialists to explore ways "to help strengthen the COSATI system from within so the libraries/information centers and federal agencies which developed, approved, and are still heavily using COSATI standards can move toward consistent interaction with other national and international bibliographic networks." Twenty-nine participants attended. Two task groups were formed. One task group was to look into who uses COSATI and write a statement that would justify its continued use, if it could be justified. The other was to study the COSATI standard for descriptive cataloging and make recommendations for improvements.

In the spring of 1978, the Working Group issued *Guidelines for Descriptive Cataloging of Reports; a Revision of COSATI Standard for Descriptive Cataloging of Government Scientific and Technical Reports*.[2] No major changes in the standard were made, but a number of minor changes to update the rules and achieve greater consistency among the users were incorporated. This report was distributed by DTIC (formerly DDC), NASA, and DOE. It was sold to the general public and abroad by NTIS and was distributed to the depository library system by GPO.

The warm reception given this first effort encouraged the Working Group to consider updating other COSATI standards, or determine the requirements for new or revised rules. Three more task groups were formed to look at the rules for (a) corporate author headings, (b) subject category codes, and (c) flagging/tagging.

Coordinated Input System Proposed

The Working Group on Updating COSATI soon concluded that a coordinated data element dictionary was needed, with standardized subsets of codes and rules. These rules, then, could be used by the four major Federal A&I services and other interested agencies and libraries. Toward this end, they prepared a proposal[3] and presented it to a group of Federal technical information managers at a meeting on December 6, 1978, in the office of Andrew A. Aines (then Special Assistant for Information Management, Office of the Under Secretary of Defense, Research and Engineering, Research and Advanced Technology). Others who attended were George Chandler (Chief, Scientific and Technical Information Branch, NASA), Joseph Coyne (Director, Technical Information Center, Department of Energy), Melvin S. Day (Director, National Technical Information Service), Hubert E. Sauter (Administrator, Defense Technical Information Center) and Ruth S. Smith (Manager, Technical Information Services, Institute for Defense Analyses, and representing the Working Group on Updating COSATI).

The proposal pointed out that to anticipate the future and plan for it, our information systems must contribute significantly to the productivity of the research programs, be sufficiently flexible to accept expected and unexpected change, feature maximum compatibility with other information systems, and accomplish these goals at the lowest investment of resources. The main thrust of the proposal was to support a coordinated input system to be used by interested government agencies and others in the indexing and abstracting of R&D projects (proposed and ongoing), report literature (completed R&D), and technical information (data).

Data Element Dictionary

The first objective outlined in the proposal was to develop projects that would assist in making these information systems more compatible, such as compilation of a data element dictionary with standardized subsets of codes and rules, based on advanced technology. The second objective was to establish a mechanism for continued support of projects developed, such as keeping up to date the data element dictionary and its subsets.

Response to Proposal

Aines led the discussion which centered on preparation for the future. The group agreed that a cooperative effort among themselves and other interested agencies, and possibly a pooling of resources to support common objectives, would be useful. A course of action was outlined, as follows:

(a) A work statement will be developed for a consultant to do a feasibility study regarding the first objective in the proposal. Considerations to be included in the study: strengths and weaknesses of information agencies who are going to participate, the problems, the cost (hidden as well as actual), benefits in present system (including problems created by change), and recommendations for improving the management of these systems, retaining some degree of control over internal systems in a decentralized but coordinated national system.

(b) NTIS will take the leadership, with cooperation of others, for a joint program and will provide the initial funding of a consultant to do the feasibility study.

(c) Consultant's report on problems, issues, direction, etc. will be reviewed by this group to determine the follow-on contract effort required.

(d) Contract effort will begin.

Later, in December, Aines met with the Committee on Information Hang-ups' Working Group on Updating COSATI. He talked about the proposal, pointing out that an explosion of databases and terminals will be the direction in the next few years; we need to take a futures posture and see how we can further the work started here; it is not wise just to improve on the present but to plan for the next five years. He said they wanted the Working Group to stay involved in the program, to begin by drafting a work statement for a consultant to do the feasibility study, and deliver it to Mel Day at NTIS. The Group did this, emphasizing the data element dictionary to make sure that it was included as a key factor in the development of a coordinated system.

Study of Cooperation in Processing

Toward the end of 1979, NTIS contracted with Madeline Henderson (consultant, formerly National Bureau of Standards) to do the study. (See her article in this issue.) The Henderson Report, *Study of Cooperation in the Processing of Technical Report Literature, to U.S. Department of Commerce, National Technical Information Service*,[4] was completed in August 1980.

The Henderson Report included an analysis of lists of data elements currently used by the major reports processing agencies of the Federal government (DTIC, DOE, NASA and NTIS). The study pointed out that although the differences among the agencies must be recognized—such as the age of each system and its supporting hardware/software capabilities, the philosophy behind the system design and subsequent modifications, and the mission responsibilities of each agency (and the resources available)—networks are better able to deliver information packaged to individual needs and to offer capabilities for manipulations and applications unheard of just ten years ago. Therefore, it behooves the reports processing community to plan ahead also to take advantage of working together on common problems, consulting together and sharing experiences. An added advantage would be the strengthened position of a unified representation of Federal technical reports processing when speaking to legislative actions, executive management directives, and information world pressures for integration of systems and services.

The study recommended that the four major reports processing agencies (a) compile a data element dictionary containing data elements currently used in their systems for the processing of technical reports, with definitions, rules for use, and tags and indicators, (b) distribute this within the community for use by those currently served by the systems or by those who might be developing similar reports processing systems, (c) use it themselves to determine if the standards currently in place need to be or could benefit from updating, modification, or further standardization, and (d) consider further standardization to foster improved coordination between this community and the library community.

Further suggestions in the study focused on a consideration of shared input processing (or source descriptive cataloging of Federal technical reports) based on the 17 data elements (or some subset of them) now common to all four systems. A shared processing data base should be designed, the study says, so the major agencies can pull off records for those reports which are their responsibility or of interest to them, for further processing into specialized data bases or as abstracting/indexing journals for widespread dissemination.

This idea also was proposed by Samuel T. Waters, Associate Director, National Agricultural Library, in another paper.[5] He suggested that the OCLC model might be applied to abstracting and indexing services. The approach would be to use the power and flexibility of an online distributive network, entering records via remote terminals into a commonly shared pool, with division of labor established to eliminate duplication. Each agency could draw records from the common pool to develop its own unique mission-oriented services.

Dr. Lee G. Burchinal, Director, Division of Science Information, National Science Foundation, in a draft paper on "Trends in Provision of U.S. Automated Bibliographic Data Bases" dated January 31, 1977, carried the idea further. He suggested this approach could also incorporate features that would strengthen private services, such as first obtaining from private sources any needed input rather than duplicate what already exists. For example, ERDA gets part of its input for its online services from the American Institute of Physics, and the National Library of Medicine contracts with Chemical Abstracts Service for part of its input. This principle could be extended across all fields now covered by government abstracting and indexing services.

Shared Bibliographic Input Experiment

In the summer of 1977 (the year that the Working Group on Updating COSATI was formed and before the Henderson study was undertaken), the Defense Technical Information Center (DTIC) and six remote online terminal sites established a Shared Bibliographic Input Experiment (SBIE) to test the feasibility of shared cataloging among DoD agencies and their contractors, using the Defense RDT&E Online System (DROLS) and the Remote Terminal Input System (RTIS) at DTIC.

The success of the shared cataloging experiment conducted by the Federal Library Committee and OCLC—which resulted in the establishment of standards, a saving in cataloging staff time and identification of sources for interlibrary loan—indicated that perhaps shared bibliographic input could be applied successfully to the cataloging of technical reports within the Defense community.

Participating Sites

The remote online sites which participated in the DTIC SBIE were: Air Force Weapons Laboratory (Kirtland AFB, NM), Army Armament R&D Command (Dover, NJ), Defense Communications Agency (Washington, DC), Defense Nuclear Agency (Washington, DC), Institute for Defense Analyses (Arlington, VA), and Naval Research Laboratory (Washington, DC). These sites represented each of the three military services, two independent DoD agencies and one Defense contractor. They also represented a wide range of library/information service situations, such as a distant location from DTIC, a new site installation, a substantial collection of non-DTIC reports, small as well as large volume of reports, manual as well as automated local systems, etc.

Management

DTIC provided the program manager, who was assisted by project managers from the participating sites. Several meetings were held with the managers and other participants to establish goals, agree upon operational procedures and assess progress. Two special task forces were appointed to identify local requirements for phase four of the experiment and to establish the criteria for evaluating the experiment.

Parameters

The experiment had to be conducted within the present capabilities of the existing DTIC system, with a minimum of additional programming. It could use the RTIS system, which had been developed to accept remote input from the Information Analysis Centers (IAC). Records input from the participating sites had to be formatted like those existing internally at DTIC, so the data was searchable by all DTIC retrieval programs. However, provision could be made for some differences: (a) each participant site was assigned a specific range of 100,000 AD numbers in the "E" range, to be used consecutively for inputs from each terminal, (b) an availability statement was provided for those reports which were not available from DTIC, and (c) a holdings symbol, transparent to all but the holder, was assigned to each of the participating sites.

Training

Catalogers and input operators from the remote sites were trained at DTIC. Training included lectures, materials, and hands-on experience, in an intensive one-week seminar. This was followed by frequent contact between DTIC staff and the sites, as well as colleague communication among the sites. Each site prepared its own manual of internal procedures.

Procedures

The test was to proceed in four phases. The first three would test bibliographic input for site-generated or site-controlled documents, as follows: Phase 1, current publications (data and copies going to DTIC); Phase 2, selected retrospective documents (data and copies going to DTIC); and Phase 3, documents not sent to DTIC (data only, including information on the controlling office, going to DTIC). Phase 4 would test the input of data for non-site-generated documents held in local collections (data only, including information on the originating office, going to DTIC).

Results

The first three phases, tested between September 1977 and April 1980, proved feasible. Quality of input was controlled by edit-audit printouts of records input by the remote sites, until the sites gained adequate experience in creating valid data. AD-E numbers were superimposed by DTIC's AD-A, -B or -C numbers after DTIC processed copies of the reports. The holdings symbols were appended by the sites to new records input as well as to records already in the DTIC file. Printouts of individual site holdings were available to each participant on request. The records were searchable online.

Phase 4 proved feasible. It could be done and was. However, the existing DTIC programs did not allow immediate duplicate checking. The result was, a number of duplicate records were generated. This called a halt to Phase 4 input by all but one of the remote sites. By January 1981, DTIC provided a programming change to improve duplicate checking and Phase 4 of the experiment was on again. It still continues.

Expansion of the Experiment

Encouraged by the initial success of the experiment, DTIC broadened participation in 1980 by accepting for training and input participation five additional remote online sites. These were: Redstone Scientific Information Center (Redstone Arsenal, AL), U. S. Command and General Staff College, Combined Arms Research Library (Fort Leavenworth, KA), U. S. Army TRADOC Library (Fort Monroe, VA), U. S. Naval

Weapons (China Lake, CA), and USAFETAC, Air Weather Service (Scott AFB, IL).

Benefits

The long-range goal of the experiment was to create a Defense Online Catalog, based at DTIC but interconnected with compatible remote systems that support local libraries/information centers, information analysis centers, and other mission-oriented information systems within the Defense community.

Each participating site is expected to benefit, as follows:

—Save time in not re-cataloging documents already in the DTIC system and sharing the intellectual effort of cataloging Defense Community reports.

—Provide direct online access to a shelf list of documents in one's own collection, without having to store these records locally, thus saving the duplicate cost of storage.

—Enable local sites to phase out maintenance of card catalogs, records of publications in progress and other duplicate files, which will provide a saving in catalog-maintenance man-hours as well as in the cost of additional equipment (and space) for expansion of the manual file.

—Save staff time and speed up the acquisition of non-DTIC documents by Defense libraries and information centers, through earlier identification of specific documents and their office of primary responsibility for release.

—Provide management information for better control of the publications produced by one's own agency or organization.

—Provide access to a richer store of bibliographic information which will enhance support of DoD studies and analyses.

The Defense Technical Information Center itself will benefit, too. It will be able to offer better services to the Defense Community. It will lessen the burden it now imposes on the community of users by requiring that they find the documents that DTIC does not have. It will increase the percentage of documents available from DTIC and thereby allow the user community to acquire documents more efficiently. By receiving cataloging information from source, DTIC will save cataloging time which can be applied to the quality control screening. This will provide the data base an additional measure of accuracy and reliability. In addition, this application of shared bibliographic input could serve as a model for the other agencies which interact with DTIC.

Follow-on to SBIE

By January 1980, the original six sites participating in SBIE realized that they would need to develop local systems, compatible with DTIC, to take care of information, such as Top Secret, intelligence and other sensitive or internal material, which could not be sent to DTIC. They asked DTIC to develop an automation model for technical library/ information centers, a completely compatible system which would enable them to interconnect with the DTIC as a centralized facility and handle automation requirements that are uniquely local.

This request pointed out,

> The need for standards for the automation of DoD technical libraries/ information centers is urgent, before any more develop systems of their own (or update old systems) which may not be compatible with DTIC and others. The more time goes by, the more money will have to be spent for these centers to realign existing systems to the chosen standard. DTIC already has demonstrated a capability and a capacity for R&D experimentation. The SBIE promised future cost-effective benefits for all participants—the sites, DTIC, and the end users. A further experiment to develop an automation model for local sites which are tied into DTIC could serve as a standard for DoD-wide implementation.[6]

The result was the DTIC assigned one of its people to investigate present systems already in use in DoD library/information centers and make a recommendation to management. This work is under way.

Another follow-on development is the Resource Sharing Advisory Group (RSAG) which was established by Sauter (Administrator of DTIC) with the encouragement of the participating sites. The purpose of the Group is to provide advice and make recommendations on matters dealing with the DTIC shared cataloging program and other resource sharing activities. The Group met for the first time in October 1980, discussed communication between DTIC and RSAG and made plans for the future. As partners in a mutual venture, this advisory group will be the "bridge" between DTIC as the centralized facility and the remote sites as the Shared Bibliographic Input moves from the status of experiment to ongoing program.

This cooperative effort between DTIC and its user libraries/information centers is being monitored closely. It's the testing ground for potential further steps in the direction of resource sharing within the Federal technical reports processing community.

Conclusion

The incentives for cooperation within this interactive community are great. The participants are both contributors to and users of each other's systems. Because all of them rely on direct access and prompt delivery of information to fulfill their basic mission, cooperative arrangements between and among them and a sharing of resources are becoming increasingly imperative.

Recent activities leading toward an updating of standards, experimenting with resource sharing, and, in general, working together to solve mutual problems reflect the growing desire among the major technical reports handling agencies, and the information centers and services which interact with them to achieve closer cooperation. To lower the costs of Federal and national information handling are national goals. The cooperative efforts within the Federal technical reports processing community, particularly their support of developing a coordinated system, which can be used by interested government agencies and others in the abstracting and indexing of research and development projects and products, are helping to achieve these goals.

REFERENCE NOTES

1. *COSATI standard for descriptive cataloging of government scientific and technical reports*. Washington, DC: Federal Council for Science and Technology, Committee on Scientific and Technical Information (COSATI); 1966.

2. *Guidelines for descriptive cataloging of reports: A revision of COSATI standard for descriptive cataloging of government scientific and technical reports*. Washington, DC: Committee on Information Hang-ups, Working Group on Updating COSATI; 1978 March; AD A050900; PB-277951.

3. *Abstracting and indexing R&D reports* (Proposal). Washington, DC: Committee on Information Hang-ups, Working Group on Updating COSATI; 1978 December 1. (unpublished).

4. Henderson, Madeline M., Contractor. *Study of cooperation in the processing of technical report literature to U. S. Department of Commerce, National Technical Information Service*. Bethesda, MD: Author; 1980 August 13. (unpublished).

5. Waters, Samuel T. Creation and use of citation data bases: A modest proposal. *Journal of the American Society for Information Science.* 26:126–127; 1975 March/April.

6. Smith, Ruth S. *An automation model for interconnecting DoD technical information facilities*. (Concept paper) Arlington, VA: Author; 1980 March 11. (unpublished).

SOME ASPECTS OF TECHNICAL REPORT PROCESSING BY FEDERAL AGENCIES

Madeline M. Henderson

ABSTRACT. Technical reports are a valuable resource of scientific and technical information, a resource which has been allowed to slip into less than maximum utility. While the processing of more traditional information sources has progressed and remarkably improved through such mechanisms as shared cataloging and online access to huge files of cataloging data, the corresponding processing of technical reports has remained relatively stagnant. Some efforts at coordinating the processing of reports have been made by the four Federal agencies responsible for the largest report collections. Additional efforts suggested in the paper include study of a common report format, more extensive shared processing of Federal documents and increased efforts towards cooperation in the Federal library network.

Introduction

In the spectrum of means and media for communicating scientific and technical information, technical reports tend to occupy the low position on the totem pole: first, published journals, then monographs, textbooks, perhaps conferences and professional society meetings, even U.S. Congressional publications, and—finally—technical reports. Yet technical reports are the first-line notice of work in progress, accomplishments, unexpected technical barriers to progress, unanticipated results, and projections of further efforts in specific programs. As such, technical reports are of value to colleagues in related areas of research as well as to those responsible for management of research through funding programs or budgeted line items. Technical reports can alert fellow scientists to results of immediate or long-range interest, and can assist program managers in allocating support to maximize benefits and minimize unnecessary duplication of effort.

Technical reports came to the fore as a means of communicating research results during the hectic 50's. The then rapidly increasing volumes of scientific and technical literature included newly important report literature (as contrasted with the conventional book and journal publications). The Office of Technical Services in the Department of Commerce was an early instrument for the management of reports collections; it has become the present-day National Technical Information Service (NTIS). The Department of Defense established its own documentation center (known as DTIC, the Defense Technical Information Center) to manage the burgeoning numbers of defense-related reports.

Madeline Henderson received the AB degree in chemistry at Emmanuel College and the MPA degree at American University. She has recently retired as Manager, ADP Information Analysis Project, Institute for Computer Sciences and Technology, National Bureau of Standards. She is now a consultant and can be reached at 5021 Alta Vista Road, Bethesda, MD 20014.

These and other reports-related activities of Federal agencies were coordinated by COSATI, the Committee on Scientific and Technical Information; its main interest was document control, reflecting the interests of its membership, most of whom headed the technical documentation programs of their agencies. COSATI accomplishments included the development of a standard for descriptive cataloging of technical reports. The agencies responsible for processing large collections of reports, particularly what are today NTIS, DTIC, Department of Energy (DOE), and National Aeronautics and Space Administration (NASA), needed a compatible set of descriptions for bibliographic information. (See the paper in this issue by Ruth Smith, for another discussion of COSATI efforts.) The standard made possible the sharing and pooling of descriptions of reports, and the establishment of the centralized announcement and distribution services of NTIS. Public access to Federal publications (especially technical reports) and data files of interest to the business, scientific and technical community is provided through the resources and products of NTIS, which include inputs from DTIC (unclassified defense reports), DOE (energy information) and NASA (space-related publications) as well as other Federal agencies with smaller collections of report literature.

At the same time that COSATI was coordinating the activities of technical documentation programs in Federal agencies, the activities in the more traditional library programs of those same agencies were also being coordinated. The Federal Library Committee (FLC) has been the focal point for such activities, through its task forces and committees working on problems common to all its members. The FLC "not only coordinates activity within the government community but serves in a very real way as a bridge between the Federal and non-Federal sectors."[1] It was evident then as now that Federal problems are comparable to problems faced by libraries throughout the nation, so Federal librarians interacted closely with their colleagues across the country.

Such was not the case with the Federal reports-processing activities. Reports literature has been dominated by the Federal government: Federal agencies produce reports themselves, and contractors to Federal agencies produce reports which are submitted to those agencies and published or distributed by them. There is not a widespread technical reports community like the nation-wide library community. As a result, while Federal libraries were participating in and taking advantage of such developments as the OCLC shared cataloging network, which has generated an online file of cataloging data for millions of items, information centers were taking only interim steps to control incoming reports while awaiting appearance of the printed volumes of reports announcement and abstract-index services from the responsible agencies.

Current Status

The interdependence and interactions within the Federal and Federally-related abstracting-indexing community are well described in Ruth Smith's article in this issue. I would like to concentrate on the lack of interactions, perhaps, between the Federal library and above-named abstracting-indexing communities. I propose to do this by reviewing a number of parallel efforts going on in each community. And I would like to discuss the topic in terms of the increasing opportunities and needs for building bridges between the parallel efforts, as well as initiating joint efforts to mutual advantage.

a) Shared Input Processing Activities: The library community's experience with shared input processing goes back 10 years or more. The Library of Congress (LC) developed the MARC implementation of the standard interchange format only slightly earlier than the COSATI implementation. In the ensuing years, however, a family of MARC formats for different types of material has been developed. The original work in data element identification has been the basis on which current utility networks have been built. Federal libraries participate in those networks through FEDLINK, the Federal Library and Information Network of the FLC. Today, FEDLINK, "which is one of more than 20 information networks that use OCLC, consists of over 300 members nationwide."[2]

Another prominent user of the OCLC utility is the Government Printing Office (GPO). The LC and GPO have been engaged in cooperative efforts to catalog all Federal documents, using MARC formats for books and serial publications, into the OCLC data base. Since the body of Federal documents includes technical reports, there is considerable duplication of effort in the processing of reports among GPO, the reports-processing agencies, and Federal libraries and information centers. (These records, in GPO *Monthly Catalog* format, are also available on tape by subscription through the MARC Delivery Service at LC.)

The shared input processing experience of the technical reports community is more recent and more limited. Again, Ruth Smith's article in this issue carries an excellent discussion of the SBIE, Shared Bibliographic Input Experiment, of DTIC. The experiment demonstrates that sharing of input activities makes information of value to defense-related research and development activities available sooner and more extensively than has been possible heretofore. In addition, DTIC finds that the participating sites are contributing information about technical reports not necessarily input to DTIC, "otherwise fugitive material."

The other reports-processing agencies should, I believe, be considering application of this experience to the total technical reports field. Both the library community's success with shared cataloging and the defense community's acceptance of shared input processing speak to the value, in terms of time and costs savings, of such resource sharing.

b) Format Reviews: In the 10 years or more since the machine readable cataloging (MARC) format was first introduced, there have been many advances in library automation and resource sharing. From the original model of one-directional distribution of MARC outward from LC, there has developed the networking situation exemplified by OCLC, "with multi-directional interchange of bibliographic data among different organizations."[3] Recognizing the problems inherent in such growth and fundamental shifts, LC concluded that certain aspects of the MARC format content and content designation would benefit from a study and re-evaluation, taking into account the experience built up through extensive use of the formats in diverse situations. Analysis is needed, in LC's opinion, to determine whether new data elements have to be added and whether some of the existing data elements are still valid in the present environment. To this end, LC contracted for a review of the entire series of MARC formats to evaluate them in terms of networking requirements, and to provide recommended specifications for change. A report from that contract effort should be available this Spring (1981).

It seemed obvious that the reports-processing community could benefit from this same approach, to review the data elements and content designators currently used by the major agencies. So a contract study was initiated, of which I was the principal investigator, resulting in a report submitted to NTIS in August 1980.[4] Unlike the MARC format review, this study was concerned with just the one COSATI implementation of descriptive cataloging rules, rather than a family of such implementations. But the study involved four different developments in that one implementation, covering the similarities and differences in ways the format had been applied over the years. The objective, as with the LC study, was to determine whether there was need for consideration of further standardization to achieve improved compatibilities so as to enhance cooperative processing.

I recommended, as a result of that study, that the major reports-processing agencies should undertake the compilation of a data element dictionary (DED) for the purpose of laying out all the data elements and their tags (content designators) now used. The dictionary would have immediate value to the managers of the reports-processing systems, in guiding decisions about further standardization requirements; and to users of the current systems, to illustrate the range of data elements available for their use.

These two parallel efforts, it seems to me, can benefit each other: examining how the other community's format evolved and changed over the same time span should point to principles fundamental to the process of document identification in today's environment, distinct from the more apparent differences in nomenclature, coding schemes, and modes of operation.

c) Minimum Bibliographic Record Studies: Another area of library experience pertinent to this discussion lies in the current efforts to develop a common communications format and a simplified bibliographic record. I lump these two efforts together, because both are concerned with core data elements and with improving cooperative processing and resource sharing. As such, they are of basic interest to the technical reports-processing function.

The Common Communication Format (CCF) is proposed to satisfy the requirements of the information and library communities. The work is being carried on by the Ad Hoc Group on the Establishment of a Common Communication Format, under UNESCO sponsorship. The group first proposed the compilation of a directory of data elements encompassing the major international formats now in use. Its relation to the DED recommended for technical reports is found, in my opinion, in the statement proposing that effort, to the effect that such a directory would provide a tool to permit the direct comparison of fields in various formats.

Five principles have been identified as the basis for developing the CCF; the one of greatest interest here is that the core record should consist of those data elements essential to the "unique identification and description of the bibliographic item identified in a standard manner." A recent effort toward identifying the core elements and the current differences in their use consisted of comparing forms of personal and corporate body (including meetings) names that appear in library cataloging records and corresponding indexing records. The object of the study was to evaluate the extent to which items are traceable when retrieving on author fields created according to different rules. More specifically, the objective was to measure the difficulties a user might encounter when attempting to find an item through a library catalog system from a citation provided by abstracting-indexing services. The results of the comparison suggest that the chances of success are very good when comparing names in the author statement in the title paragraph of an LC/ISBD (International Standard Bibliographic Description) record with the name entry in the index service record. Comparisons were not so high when the match was tried between the same index service entries and the formalized forms in LC main and added entry fields. The results suggest to me, at least, that the search for a common communication format can be successful, that room for compromise and agreement exists.

The minimal level cataloging studies propose as a subset of national level bibliograpic records (as contrasted with the international scope of the CCF effort) specifications for data elements that will identify an item without incurring the costs of full bibliographic description. The effort here is to specify the data elements considered essential for such identifications. This is, I suggest, an effort far removed from traditional insistence on complete cataloging based on rigid requirements, and is perhaps a measure of where advancing technologies and (always) shrinking economic resources lead us.

In my study conducted for the reports-processing community, reviewing the COSATI format, I recommended that when the DED has been compiled, system managers concentrate their review on the relatively small number of data elements used by all four systems. These elements, I suggested, are sufficient to identify documents but may not constitute all the elements necessary to accomplish the control operations and the production of printed services by individual agencies. These core elements could, for example, be the ones studied for further standardization efforts, at least initially. They also could be the ones emphasized in cooperative processing activities. (I'll discuss this point more fully in the next section.) In those contexts, the data elements common to the reports-processing systems parallel the elements under consideration in the CCF and minimal-level cataloging studies.

To recap, activities pertinent to this discussion include: in the reports-processing community, the review of current formats used by DOE, NASA, DTIC, and NTIS, to determine the need for further standardization, and the DTIC's Shared Bibliographic Input Experiment; in the library community, review of MARC formats, examination of the Common Communications Format and minimal level cataloging provisions, and the GPO-LC cooperation in cataloging Federal documents.

Emerging Opportunities

In addition to the activities discussed above, which I characterize as parallel within the two communities but not interacting between them, there are other developments of interest to this essay.

One is the study, sponsored by the FLC and the NCLIS (National Commission on Libraries and Information Science), to improve coordination of resources and services among Federal and non-Federal libraries and information centers in a developing nationwide library and information service network. A major component of such a network is the community of Federal libraries and information centers, which comprises extensive collections of materials distributed among 2,300 libraries and information centers across the country. The coordination of their resources and services, not only within the Federal structure but also with the public at local, state, and regional levels, is essential for an effective nationwide program. The study is now underway, assessing current interactions among Federal libraries and centers and between Federal and non-Federal sectors, with the view to developing guidelines and recommendations to achieve the integration of the Federal units into the developing nationwide network. The library and reports-processing communities are, of course, both represented in those Federal libraries and information centers.

Another development of interest is the assignment of responsibility to GPO, under the National Publications Act, for prescription of minimum bibliographic and indexing standards for Federal documents and, indeed, for the bibliographic processing of all Federal documents. As noted above, GPO has been inputting the cataloging of the documents it prints into the OCLC data base; from this, it produces its monthly catalog, and of course the catalog record is available to the Federal libraries who participate in shared cataloging through OCLC. To discharge its responsibility for processing all Federal documents, GPO has heretofore relied on NTIS abstracting-indexing, and its *Government Reports Announcement and Index*, to cover all documents it (GPO) did not process.

Now GPO is concerned that the non-GPO processing is not available to Federal librarians through OCLC for their online access. Staff at GPO have begun discussions with staff at NTIS, concerning the possibility of making the NTIS records so available to Federal librarians. However, the problem is not simple: NTIS tapes are in COSATI format and OCLC cataloging is done in MARC format. Conversion is not a one-to-one proposition. But this situation invites the kind of bridging and joint ventures I referred to earlier in this paper.

Still another development pertinent to this discussion is the appearance of a MARC format for technical reports. Having just appeared in a reasonably final form, the format has not been tested or examined under the contract study for LC, nor has it figured in the cataloging of Federal documents by GPO or the indexing of technical reports by NTIS and the other major reports-processing agencies. However, it deserves consideration as a tool for describing such items, in light of the other developments we've mentioned.

a) *Data Element Dictionary:* The recommendation to NTIS and the other agencies, as a result of the study of their reports-processing formats, called for preparation of a directory (or dictionary) containing all the data elements currently used in their systems, at least for the processing of technical reports, and including definitions, rules for use, and the tags and indicators applicable to the elements. If possible, the DED could encompass all the data elements in current use for whatever documents or items (journal articles, conference proceedings, etc.).

As a result of the discussions between GPO and NTIS an effort will be made to try to expand that dictionary to include the MARC formats used by GPO in its OCLC cataloging, and—perhaps—the new MARC format for technical reports. These constitute meaningful extensions to the original proposal, of course, and complicate the compilation in a measurable way. But the thought is that there exists at this time an opportunity for a joint effort for mutual benefit.

I have heard described, by a colleague who had "lived through it," the value of laying out data elements from a number of related files (or systems, in this case), side by side for comparison, thus seeing the variations in the way similar data are handled, and the resulting efficiencies realized by standardizing on the handling of those elements. The recommendation for compilation of the DED for technical reports called further for consideration of standardizing not only the data elements but also their tags/indicators. The latter is important, because tags are a visible and integral part of the way data elements are recorded; standardization would result in a uniform appearance to a Federal reports bibliographic data processing system. And the more easily these tags interface in form with the systems of other sectors, e.g., the library community's MARC-based tags, the better is the chance for effecting broader system interfaces as well.

b) *Shared Input Processing of Federal Documents:* The recommendations to NTIS, as noted above, included consideration of possible further standardization of data elements and their tags/indicators, primarily to improve cooperative processing among the major agencies involved. But there also comes the opportunity, in my opinion, for the agencies to redirect their resources from their in-house input processing to their products and service functions. One way to accomplish this is to provide for shared input processing by the libraries and information centers in agency laboratories or in contractors' laboratories where the technical reports are generated or processed. In other words, the technical reports community should follow the example of the library community in its successful shared cataloging experience.

I spoke earlier of suggesting that the agencies consider focusing on those data elements which are common to their systems, which are sufficient to identify their documents though perhaps not all that are necessary to fulfill their mission responsibilities (printed indexes, sales, etc.).

Now an experiment is being considered in the shared input processing of Federal documents, which seeks to combine the sharing aspects with the common data elements idea. Federal documents include the whole range from books and serials to technical reports, i.e., what GPO now catalogs and what the four agencies abstract and index.Basing the shared processing on a set of core elements identified through the DED exercise described above, will, it is believed, make for easier training, better quality control, and increased efficiency in processing. More than that, basing the experiment on a small set of data elements provides a fighting chance for agreement on forms, standards, conventions, rules—all the good things we need to make the experiment start, no less fly.

The design of this experimental shared-processing data base will allow the participants in the experiment to identify records for those documents which are their responsibility, or in which they are interested, for further processing into specialized data bases or for publication and dissemination through catalogs or indexes.

Others, of course, are experimenting with the use of records containing basic data, or preliminary cataloging. What will be tried here is the identification of documents in a minimal format that will permit expansion either to library-type cataloging or abstracting/indexing detail. The benefits would include early announcement of available documents and reduced duplication of the effort now expended in Federal documents processing.

Conclusion

Whether the experiment can succeed remains to be seen; the challenge will be to knit together all these strands of activities and interests that are running parallel or seemingly converging. It must be recognized that such developments, and the planned effort just described, entail obligations and responsibilities which are binding on the participants, and preclude some unilateral actions at times. And complete development of this kind of utility may be a long way off. But it is hoped that the effort might be laying the ground for improvements in the efficiency and effectiveness of Federal technical reports processing and, therefore, of their utilization.

REFERENCE NOTES

1. Henderson, Madeline M. The Federal sector. In: Hammer, Donald P., ed. *The information age: its development, its impact*. Metuchen, N.J.: Scarecrow Press; 1976: p. 100.
2. FEDLINK and Agency field libraries. *FLC Newsletter*. 118:1; 1980 December.
3. *LC Information Bulletin*. 464; 1979 November 9.
4. Henderson, Madeline M., Contractor. *Study of cooperation in the processing of the technical report literature to U.S. Department of Commerce, National Technical Information Service*. Bethesda, MD: Author; 1980 August 13. (unpublished).

MANAGING THE BELL LABORATORIES TECHNICAL REPORT SERVICE

Amy Wang
Diane M. Alimena

ABSTRACT. The Technical Report Service (TRS) of Bell Laboratories uses a computer-driven, microfiche-based system to manage its technical report collection and services. This paper presents an overview of TRS systems and services, including its methods of acquiring, announcing, and distributing technical reports, and providing specialized reference and retrieval services to a large, sophisticated user community.

Introduction

To maintain responsive services and efficient operations, the Bell Laboratories Technical Report Service (TRS) must pay close attention to data on report circulation, as well as ordering, retention, announcement, and distribution policies. The collection size and the volume of requests handled require automated techniques to collect and evaluate use data. TRS has developed computer-driven, microfiche-based services featuring fast service response, automated data collection and statistical analysis feedback systems. To understand how its systems and services work, the organization TRS serves and the information environment within which it functions must be reviewed.

Bell Laboratories, the research and development unit of the Bell System, is based at 17 locations in eight states. Some 22,000 employees, including 10,500 scientists and engineers, and 5,000 technical assistants, work primarily in telecommunications-related fields, designing and developing communications equipment for manufacture by Western Electric (the manufacturing and distributing arm of the Bell System), and designing networks and operations services to support the Bell Telephone Operating Companies.

Because their work ranges from pure research to process development for equipment manufacture, Bell Labs employees demand information over a wide range of subjects: chemistry, physics, electronics, electrical and mechanical engineering, computer science, mathematics, management, and behavioral sciences. To help meet these information needs, the single library, created when Bell Labs was formed in 1925, has

---

Amy Wang is Group Supervisor, Technical Report Service, at Bell Laboratories, Whippany Road, Whippany, NJ 07891. She received an AB degree from Bryn Mawr College and the MLS degree from Rutgers University. Diane M. Alimena is Reference Librarian at the Bell Laboratories Technical Library, 600 Mountain Ave., Murray Hill, NJ 07974. She received the BA degree (mathematics) at Montclair State College and the MLS degree from Rutgers University.

evolved into the Bell Labs Library Network, a complex of more than two dozen libraries and specialized information service units, sharing resources, responsibilities, and systems.[1,2]

Technical Report Service: An Overview

As its name implies, the business of the Technical Reports Service is technical reports—acquiring, announcing, storing and supplying the technical documents required to support both short- and long-term Bell Labs research and development needs, and providing reference, literature searching, and report consulting services to answer specific requests for information. TRS focuses on external documents; a separate service, also part of the Library Network, is responsible for internal technical information.

As one of the Network's centralized services, TRS serves all Bell Laboratories from a single location—in this case, Whippany, N.J. Centralization of specialized services permits development of the critical mass of required expertise and mechanisms. Moreover, considering the large number of reports issued each year, the transient nature of the information they contain, and their numerous sources and announcement publications, a centralized collection provides the most cost-effective and efficient means of handling technical reports. The TRS report collection, carefully defined to match Bell Labs information requirements, is, of course, only a small subset of available technical reports; it currently includes 145,000 titles and grows at a rate of 19,000 titles annually. Over 85% of the reports are in microfiche form, the remaining portion in paper form.

TRS Report Collection

Nature of Technical Reports

Although technical reports are the daily concern of many information services, many technical librarians have had little experience with this class of "unpublished" literature. Government, academic, research and industrial institutions produce technical reports to announce the status of projects or the results of completed research; many organizations produce them specifically to meet the requirements of a contract or grant. Since they are frequently unpublished or informally produced (mimeographed or photocopied versions of handwritten or typed notes), reports are often the first publically available information on a project or research. Moreover, although the same information may appear later in a journal article, monograph, or conference paper, a report is often free or relatively inexpensive.

The special nature of technical reports creates unique problems in their acquisition and control:

—The sheer volume of reports produced in the U.S. alone would inundate any collection, unless one selected reports carefully.
—Countless organizations generate technical reports. As many as three

types of institutions may be involved in the creation and distribution of one report: (1) institutions performing the research, (2) sponsoring agencies, and (3)distributing agencies. Both sponsoring and distributing agencies may control the distribution and accessibility of reports according to differing standards; the producing agency may also directly distribute reports. Thus, availability varies widely for each report, and from institution to institution.

—Not only do many institutions produce reports irregularly, but often they do not index or even announce the availability of completed reports. It is sometimes not clear who sponsored a report, or when it originated.

—Conventional abstracting and indexing publications, and other bibliographic services, frequently are of little aid in identifying technical reports.

—The report number format varies according to the specifications of each sponsoring institution, usually having some internal significance. Not only the sponsoring institution, but also the producing and the distributing agencies (if different), may assign other report numbers to the same document. Adding to the confusion, a grant or contract number may also appear on the report.

—Reports often go out of print shortly after publication. Because of the transient nature of the information they contain (especially if they belong to a series of progress reports), and because of budget constraints, many institutions will not reprint reports.

Receiving reports via automatic distribution solves some of the acquisition and control problems. However, one must first identify those institutions that may provide the most useful reports, and then determine the qualification for inclusion on their automatic distribution lists. Even when one can receive reports automatically, there still is a problem: many institutions distribute reports only by series, and many series are a heterogenous lot, mixing many different subject areas.

TRS Report Sources

In general, TRS is responsible for collecting reports from any outside agency or institution on subjects relevant to Bell Labs research. Much of the collection is acquired from the National Technical Information Service (NTIS), an agency of the U.S. Department of Commerce. NTIS functions as "the central source for the public sale of Government-sponsored research, development and engineering reports and other analyses prepared by Federal agencies, their contractors or grantees, or by special technology groups."[3] NTIS announces its new acquisitions every two weeks in its *Government Reports Announcements and Index (GRA)*.

GRA classifies reports using the 1964 COSATI (Committee on Scientific and Technical Information of the Federal Council for Science and Technology) classification scheme, and indexes citations by keyword, personal and corporate author, contract/grant number, and NTIS report number. Although *GRA* announced reports can be ordered individually in either microfiche or paper copy, the selective dissemination of information service of NTIS, Selected Research in Microfiche (SRIM), is a more efficient acquisition system. Through SRIM, TRS acquires thousands of fiche-copy reports (17,175 in 1980) cost-effectively. For each *GRA* issue, SRIM automatically provides TRS with microfiche copies of reports according to its subject profile. In use since 1970, the NTIS profile codes, which do not coincide with COSATI codes, consist of 38 main categories, each divided into 4 to 27 subcategories.

Although NTIS provides excellent access to more than a million reports (their present collection exceeds 1,200,000 reports and they acquire 80,000 a year), currently it distributes primarily U.S. Government-sponsored reports. Since this limits the number of potentially useful reports NTIS handles, TRS also independently solicits reports from other sources in the United States, Europe, the Far East, and other areas.

TRS Collection Organization

Document format and security requirements divide the TRS collection into three physically distinct groups: (1) unclassified fiche copy reports, (2) unclassified paper copy reports, and (3) classified reports. Although the three require different storage facilities, they are filed similarly within each group.

Since locating or shelving reports arranged by report number is easier than finding or filing those arranged by author or title, TRS files its collection by report number. Because NTIS supplies 85% of the collection, and because TRS relies primarily on the *GRA* index to identify reports, documents are arranged by the NTIS report number, rather than a sponsoring agency's number. Three exceptions to that rule exist:

—Reports without an NTIS-assigned number.
—Reports that belong to a well-known, often-referred-to, series, such as Rand Papers and Reports.
—Reports, with an NTIS-number longer than 11 characters, that TRS has announced in its biweekly current awareness report announcement bulletin, *Current Technical Reports (CTR)*, described elsewhere in this paper.

When a report does not have an NTIS number, TRS assigns a 7-character one in the following form:

XXyyyyy

where yyyyy is a sequentially-assigned 5-digit number.

Using a standardized, TRS-assigned report number offers the following advantages over using the performing, sponsoring, or distributing agency numbers:

—The TRS cataloger does not have to decide which of several report numbers to use.

—It simplifies shelving and locating reports.
—The number format lies within acceptable parameters for the software packages producing *CTR*, and its computerized request processing system.
—It immediately identifies the report as a non-NTIS item, a part of the TRS miscellaneous document collection.

TRS indexes XX reports in an internally produced and maintained XX Index, that is described elsewhere in this paper.

Series of reports, such as those issued by the MIT Artificial Intelligence Laboratory, may have NTIS numbers, as well as issuing agency report numbers. If requesters often refer to them by series name or number, and if TRS holds a significant part of the series, then they are filed according to the issuing agency number, increasing the speed of document identification and location. When a document from a series also has an NTIS number, it is cross-referenced by the NTIS number in the fiche files. Report series constitute one-third of the miscellaneous document collection, and appear in the XX Index.

When TRS announces, in *CTR*, a document with an NTIS report number exceeding 11 characters, the computerized announcement system assigns it a 10-character report number, in the following format:

ZZ-wwxxyyy,

where

ww = last two digits of the year of the *CTR* issue announcing the report

xx = *CTR* issue number

yyy = a 3-digit, sequentially-assigned number.

Cross reference between the original NTIS number and the ZZ-number appear in the fiche file.

Classified reports constitute a very small portion of the reports handled through TRS. They are not announced or distributed as described above. Classified reports are acquired only as a result of specific requests, and, immediately after receipt, assigned to the technical organization requesting them. Classified documents are ordered through the Defense Technical Information Center (DTIC) and, for the brief time TRS is responsible for them, they are stored by DTIC report numbers in a security vault.

Current Awareness Service

Besides acting as the Network's depository for externally produced technical reports, TRS has the equally important if not more important, function of keeping Bell Labs employees aware of new, relevant reports. *Current Technical Reports (CTR)*, a 20-to 40-page biweekly publication, announces 250 to 300 newly acquired reports to 3300 subscribers. Announcement in *CTR* generates 88% of the requests for some 4000 of the reports that employees order through TRS each month. (Figure 1)

CURRENT TECHNICAL REPORTS

MARCH 30, 1981
CTR 7

CONTENTS

Chemistry
Communications
Computer Science and Technology
Earth and Space Sciences
Electrical Engineering
    Devices and Components
    Subsystems
Energy
Life Sciences
Management, Marketing and Economics
Materials Science
Mathematics and Operations Research
Mechanical and Industrial Engineering
Physics
    Acoustics
    Optics
    Solid State
    Physics - Other
Miscellaneous Reports

Bell Laboratories LIBRARY NETWORK

Figure 1. Front Cover of *CTR*, Displaying Subject Categories.

To produce a current awareness bulletin one must first identify the audience's interests. Although it is impossible to know all of Bell Lab's research interests, the TRS staff keeps abreast of the general areas of interest and new technical developments by scanning and reviewing Bell Labs publications. The staff also identifies and examines specific areas of research through the TRS Technical Contact Program, a system of informal interviews with Bell Labs technical experts. A relatively brief interview with a Labs authority in a particular field, or with the representative of a Bell Labs organization, indicates what subjects specifically interest an organization, or which parts of a field appear most useful to Bell Labs research, and, equally important, which aspects are not of interest. Even normal, daily contacts—spontaneous discussions with people ordering reports, phone calls from colleagues, lunchtime conversations, etc.—provide the TRS staff with additional guidance for *CTR* selection.

CTR Production

As soon as it arrives, the staff scans each *GRA* issue for reports of interest to Bell Labs, deleting most interim reports, some foreign language ones, those published as journal articles, and reports NTIS identifies as illegible. Additionally, the TRS staff examines any recently received non-NTIS reports for possible inclusion in *CTR* and either prepares an abstract or chooses key words to describe the subject of the non-NTIS documents. To every report selected for announcement, the staff assigns one of seventeen *CTR* subject categories.

To generate *CTR*, TRS uses an IBM 370 computer system in conjunction with BELLTAB, a PL/1 software package developed by Bell Labs in 1971. This system uses the NTIS magnetic tape that corresponds to each *GRA* issue, as input. From the citations of reports selected from *GRA* issues, the staff, using an interactive, online computer editing system, creates a file of the NTIS report numbers and the *CTR* subject categories assigned to each report. BELLTAB then searches the NTIS magnetic tape for the citations associated with those report numbers, and creates a disc file, containing the complete abstract for each report chosen and the desired information from the citation. To enter non-NTIS documents, TRS creates a separate file: entered from each document are the report number (the original, for series of reports, or an internally assigned ZZ- or XX number), title, author, corporate author, *CTR* subject category, and either keywords or an abstract.

Next, BELLTAB combines the NTIS and non-NTIS files and sorts the report citations, first by subject, then by report number, producing a file that contains a sorted, formatted list of report citations. Finally, BELLTAB produces a camera-ready master copy of *CTR* that is sent to an outside printer. Producing the camera-ready copy usually takes a week; printing copies for and distributing them to subscribers takes two weeks.

The *CTR* production system also affects three of the twelve centralized current awareness bulletins produced by the Bell Labs Library Network. Using the *CTR* subject categories, BELLTAB identifies report citations in computer science, life science, and management literature, and transmits a copy of those citations to three separate computer files. Editors of the three awareness bulletins—*Current Management Literature,* the *Life Sciences Bulletin,* and the *Computing Information Bulletin*—review the contents of the appropriate file, and select relevant citations for inclusion in their publication. By using an interactive, online computer system to edit the contents of the appropriate file, the editors produce a printed version of the selected citations for their bulletin production systems.

Request Processing System

CTR subscribers record their requests for reports on the back cover of *CTR* (Figure 2) as they scan the issue, indicating their preference for either paper or microfiche copy. After receiving the forms back in the company mail, TRS uses an interactive computer editing system to enter the employee ID number, report numbers, and a code indicating the requester's preference for paper or microfiche copy. A request program sorts the data to produce a report referral list of requested documents in report number order, indicating the number of copies ordered in fiche, or paper format. It also generates an address card for each document a requester orders, with the report number, and the requester's name and company mailing address.

Using the report referral list generated by the request program, the staff gathers the microfiche copies of requested reports from the TRS files. When requesters order microfiche copies, TRS duplicates the microfiche on an NB Printer and Processor 404A diazo system for the requester's permanent retention. Paper copies of reports are generated from the TRS microfiche using a Xerox 970 Microfiche Printing System.

Instead of addressing envelopes for each document TRS mails to requesters, the staff uses the address card that the request program created. The cards are stapled to each paper copy of a report or to the envelope containing a fiche copy of a report, and the documents are placed in the company mail.

CTR Selection Feedback

One advantage of an automated bulletin production and request processing systems is the statistical feedback it generates. TRS relies on two specially designed statistics programs to help determine if *CTR* announces an efficient ratio of relevant documents.

Each quarter TRS runs a program that examines the requests generated by the *CTR* issues produced in that period. The program lists, in subject category order, the titles that have had more than 10 requests (Figure 3), and those that no one ordered (Figure 4). In addition, it presents a statistical summary of the titles selected by requesters ("hits") versus the number of titles announced in each category of the *CTR* issues being studied. (Figure 5).

Each year another program examines the number of titles requested

TECHNICAL REPORT SERVICE
WH 5E 227
March 2, 1981
CTR 5

CURRENT TECHNICAL REPORTS

Complete only if information is different from that on the label above. (Address information is supplied to us automatically from the Telephone Directory Group.)

_____   _____
Name   Payroll Account Number

* * * * * * *

☐ Add my name to the CURRENT TECHNICAL REPORTS distribution list.
☐ Remove my name from the distribution list.

* * * * * * *

Send me reports having the following numbers:

Paper Copy		Microfiche Copy

Figure 2. *CTR* Order Form.

by each Bell Labs organization within each *CTR* subject category. The statistics also show how many reports requesters ordered in paper form and how many in microfiche. (Figure 6)

Each statistical report acts as a yardstick of the staff's success in selecting reports for announcement in *CTR*, and of their judgement in categorizing those titles by a particular subject. A low "hit" rate cate-

THE FOLLOWING REPORTS IN CATEGORY 08 WERE REQUESTED 10 OR MORE TIMES

REQUESTS	REPORT NO.	TITLE	CTR NO.
17	AD-A086457	HUMAN DECISION-MAKING IN COMPUTER AIDED FAULT	26
12	AD-A086468	BIOLOGICAL EFFECTS OF NONIONIZING ELECTROMAGNETIC	26
21	AD-A086514	INTELLIGENCE AND NONENTRENCHMENT.	26
12	AD-A086797	CLAIMS, COUNTERCLAIMS, AND COMPONENTS: A	26
29	AD-A086796	REASONING, PROBLEM SOLVING, AND INTELLIGENCE.	26
21	AD-A086592	AN ANNOTATED SELECTIVE BIBLIOGRAPHY ON HUMAN	26
19	AD-A086057	INDIVIDUAL DIFFERENCE RELATIONS IN PSYCHOMETRIC AND	25
26	AD-A086064	JOB SATISFACTION.	25
18	AD-A085917	RESEARCH IN NATURAL LANGUAGE UNDERSTANDING.	25
20	AD-A085997	CONCEPTS, PROPOSITIONS, AND SCHEMATA: WHAT ARE THE	25
15	AD-A085985	FINGER MOVEMENTS IN TRANSCRIPTION TYPING.	25
17	AD-A085894	PROBLEM SOLVING IN A NATURAL LANGUAGE ENVIRONMENT.	25
20	AD-A085824	HUMAN PERFORMANCE: PSYCHOLOGICAL AND PHYSIOLOGICAL SEX	25
13	AD-A086405	THE INFLUENCE OF LEARNING STRATEGIES IN THE	26
10	AD-A086288	MAGNETIC FIELDS OF THE CEREBRAL CORTEX.	26
24	AD-A086139	HUMAN ENGINEERING DESIGN CRITERIA FOR MODERN	25
11	PB80-177165	TOWARDS USABLE USER STUDIES: ASSESSING THE INFORMATION	21
31	PB80-176845	ON 1012: A CHECK ON EARTH CARRYING CAPACITY FOR MAN.	21
11	N80-23985	CLARIFICATION PROCESS: RESOLUTION OF DECISION-PROBLEM	22
14	LBL-10527	IMPACT OF REDUCED VENTILATION ON INDOOR AIR QUALITY IN	24
13	ZZ-802417	HEALTH EFFECTS OF LOW LEVEL RADIATION.	24
11	PB80-195688	THE STRUCTURE OF WITHDRAWAL: RELATIONSHIPS AMONG	24
15	AD-A083973	COMPREHENSION AND ANALYSIS OF INFORMATION IN TEXT. II	21
61	AD-A083980	WORK AND ORGANIZATIONAL LIFE IN THE YEAR 2000.	21
14	AD-A084141	MEMORY ORGANIZATION AND SEARCH PROCESSES FOR	22
35	AD-A083798	THE FRAMING OF DECISIONS AND THE RATIONALITY OF	21
12	AD-A083686	AN ANNOTATED BIBLIOGRAPHY ON OPERATOR MENTAL WORKLOAD	21
26	AD-A084866	LIFE STRESS AND COPING SKILLS IN RELATION TO	23
12	AD-A084821	A SELECTED DESCRIPTOR-INDEXED BIBLIOGRAPHY TO THE	23
52	AD-A084754	ACQUISITION OF A MEMORY SKILL.	23
14	AD-A084723	SYMPOSIUM ON THE RECOGNITION AND CLASSIFICATION OF	22
19	AD-A084383	THE ADVANTAGE OF THE COLOR-CODE MODALITY VERSUS	22
32	AD-A084617	A CONCEPT FOR DEVELOPING HUMAN PERFORMANCE	22
17	AD-A084551	A FIVE-STAGE MODEL OF THE MENTAL ACTIVITIES INVOLVED	22
21	AD-A085597	A STUDY OF FLEXITIME EFFECTS IN A GOVERNMENT RESEARCH	24
36	AD-A085659	VALIDITY OF LEARNING STRATEGIES/SKILLS TRAINING.	24

Figure 3. Sample Statistics Program Output: Titles with 10 or More Requests.

gory, i.e., one in which requesters chose only a few titles, determines the next area for a Technical Contact Program interview. Fields with "hit" rates that are too high suggest that *CTR* may not be offering subscribers enough choices. According to previous experience, an 80-85% "hit" rate in any category implies good selection.[4]

Reference Service

Most TRS reference work falls into two categories: literature searching, and document identification and location. Additionally, TRS assists the other Bell Labs libraries and individual requesters in locating or learning about obscure government, private, public, foreign, and domestic institutions that produce or distribute technical reports. When requested, TRS collects information (address, subject expertise, report distribution procedures, etc.) on those organizations. Thus, TRS acts as consultant, liaison, and information center for Bell Labs on technical reports.

Reference Sources

Since NTIS provides access to such a large collection of reports, TRS considers the NTIS index, *GRA*, a major reference source. However, TRS also depends on the following abstracts and indexes for access to report literature and sources:

—*Scientific and Technical Aerospace Reports* (STAR), published by the National Aeronautics and Space Administration (NASA). It announces and indexes NASA produced or sponsored reports, and any reports or translations (issued in report form) from other U.S. government agencies, and domestic and foreign institutions, that fall within the area of aeronautics, space science, and supporting disciplines.

—*Technical Abstract Bulletin* (TAB), published by the DTIC. TAB describes classified and unclassified documents that cannot be released to the general public; document classification ranges from confidential to secret.

—Indexes and abstracts of report series issued by private institutions, such as the *Selected Rand Abstracts,* and the *Stanford Electronic Lab—Bibliography of Technical Reports.*

—XX Index, an internally produced and maintained index of 20,000 non-NTIS reports housed in the TRS collection. Produced by BELDEX (a Bell Labs indexing program), using the report numbering scheme already described above, the Index provides personal, corporate author, report number, issuing agency, and permuted title access to miscellaneous reports.

Online Systems

As so many other information services do, TRS relies heavily on online database searching systems to locate citations and other information. The NTIS database, essentially an online version of the *GRA*, is the major TRS resource for literature searches. This database covers reports distributed by NTIS from 1964 to the present. TRS uses several other databases, as well, including the Government Printing Office (GPO) Monthly Catalog, and the Congressional Information Service (CIS), to enhance its information retrieval service.

Naturally, document location and address searching also benefit from the use of online searching, especially since the corporate source field is fully searchable on most databases. In addition, TRS uses the OCLC system to identify, locate, and request interlibrary photocopies or loans of reports that TRS cannot obtain through other channels.

Challenges and Opportunities for TRS

To remain responsive to needs of its audience, any service must seek improvement. Thus, both as an individual information center, and as a specialized unit of the Bell Labs Library Network, TRS is investigating new means of enhancing its systems and services. Potential systems include electronic delivery of report current awareness services, elec-

THE FOLLOWING REPORTS IN CATEGORY 08 WERE NOT REQUESTED

ACCESSION NO.	TITLE	CTR NO.
PB80-192966	A FIELD INVESTIGATION OF NOISE REDUCTION AFFORDED BY	24
PB80-191505	COLLECTION AND ANALYSIS OF WORK SURFACE ACCIDENT	23
AD-A084086	SIZE, DISTANCE, AND PERIPHERAL POSITION EFFECTS ON	22
AD-A084121	MUTAGENICITY AND DNA REPAIR POTENTIAL OF 15 CHEMICALS.	22
AD-A083720	HAZARDS/FAILURE MODES AND EFFECTS ANALYSIS MK 1 MOD 0	21
AD-A083855	FIRST-GENERATION NUMERICAL OCEAN PREDICTION MODELS --	21
AD-A083654	MOORED ACOUSTIC TRAVEL TIME (ATT) CURRENT METERS:	21
AD-A084409	ATTENUATION VARIATION OBTAINED WITH TRAINING WHEN	22
AD-A085737	A PILOT STUDY OF EXPERIMENTER-SUBJECT EFFECT ON DARK	24

Figure 4. Sample Statistics Program Output: Titles Not Requested.

tronic mail of intra-Network requests from all locations, and increasing the range of report documents available through the Network.

Although TRS already offers Bell Labs access to thousands of reports, it plans to develop further systems to announce and distribute several additional classes of documents to improve Network coverage:

—College and university reports
—Scientific and technical documents from the Government Printing Office (GPO)
—Copyrighted technical reports.

Because so many academic institutions distribute reports, TRS intends to develop a systematic method of identifying and obtaining college or university reports, especially in the area of computer science. Individual departments of an institution often distribute their reports independently of and unknown to one another and this complicates the situation. Thus, obtaining academic reports resembles an attempt to acquire reports from all government agencies, without using NTIS.

Today, just as they did for reports before the existence of TRS, the libraries and information centers of the Network individually select, acquire, and retain GPO documents. The GPO not only prints material for federal agencies, but also acts as the sales and distribution office for many of their documents. Although many GPO-distributed documents qualify as technical reports, NTIS distributes a few of them. Many agencies seem to overlook it as a distribution center for their out-of-print reports. Moreover, the GPO documents that NTIS does distribute usually appear in their files months after the GPO announced them. While GPO reports, containing information potentially useful to Bell Labs, represent only a small fraction of those TRS receives from NTIS, developing a system of acquiring useful GPO documents would save much time in identifying and obtaining them.

Copyrighted reports present another problem not easily resolved. Since its request processing system is based primarily on reproducing copies of reports, TRS cannot satisfy large numbers of requests for

REQUEST STATISTICS FOR REPORTS 21-26 OF 1980

CATEGORY	REPORTS ANNOUNCED	REPORTS REQUESTED	% REQUESTED	TOTAL REQUESTS	REQ/REPORT ANNOUN	REQ/REPORT REQ
1	92	60	65.2	175	1.9	2.9
2	105	95	90.4	755	7.1	7.9
3	269	243	90.3	4592	17.0	18.8
4	83	58	69.8	183	2.2	3.1
5	49	44	89.7	217	4.4	4.9
6	89	67	75.2	233	2.6	3.4
7	134	113	84.3	509	3.7	4.5
8	120	111	92.4	1003	8.3	9.0
9	45	42	93.3	463	10.2	11.0
10	97	66	68.0	208	2.1	3.1
11	205	169	82.4	827	4.0	4.8
12	56	38	67.8	141	2.5	3.7
13	29	25	86.2	80	2.7	3.1
14	56	43	76.7	211	3.7	4.9
15	32	27	84.3	136	4.2	5.0
16	94	32	34.0	65	0.6	2.0
17	10	8	79.9	39	3.8	4.8
UNCLASSIFIED TOTALS	1565	1241	79.2	9837	6.2	7.9

Figure 5. Sample Statistics Program Output: Selection ("Hit") Rate.

SUMMARY OF REQUESTS FROM
CURRENT TECHNICAL REPORTS FOR 1980

CENTER 535

SUBJECT CATEGORY	NO. OF PAPER COPIES	NO. OF MICROFICHE COPIES	NO. OF REQUESTS
CHEMISTRY	0	6	6
COMMUNICATIONS	3	3	6
COMPUTING AND INFORMATION PROCESSING	88	64	152
EARTH SCIENCES, OCEANOGRAPHY, ASTRONOMY	25	36	61
ELECTRICAL ENGINEERING - SUBSYSTEMS	1	1	2
ENERGY	1	3	4
LIFE SCIENCES	8	8	16
MANAGEMENT	3	4	7
MATHEMATICS, STATISTICS, OPERATIONS RESEARCH	7	28	35
PHYSICS - OTHER	1	1	2
MISCELLANEOUS	2	0	2
TOTAL CENTER 535	139	154	293

Figure 6. Sample Output: Number of Titles Ordered from Each Subject Category by Members of a Bell Labs Organization.

copyrighted documents. Consideration will be given to expanding the request processing system to accommodate loans of reports, and to investigating, through organizations such as the Copyright Clearance Center (CCC), mechanisms for photocopying popular series reports.

Conclusion

Considering the increasing number of documents our society produces, the rapid changes in our technology, and the need of business and research centers to exploit existing research in an era of diminishing resources, information centers, such as TRS, must not only respond to and anticipate user needs, but must take fullest advantage of all information sources, and adapt their systems and procedures to benefit from any technological advances.

REFERENCE NOTES

1. Kennedy, Robert A. Bell Laboratories Library Network. In: Gibson, Robert W., Jr., ed. *The special library role in networks*. New York: Special Libraries Association; 1980: 17-36.
2. Fortney, Virginia J. The Computing Information Service Network in Bell Laboratories. To be published in *Science & Technology Libraries*. 1(2); 1980 Winter.
3. Josephs, Melvin J. Information dissemination with microforms. *IEEE Transactions on Professional Communication*. 18(3): 164–167; 1975 September.
4. English, Eileen W. Hits and misses. *Special Libraries*. 66(5-6): 237-240; 1975 May-June.

RECENT FID PUBLICATIONS

FID DIRECTORY 1981-1982
The Hague, FID, 1981, 78 p., (FID 600) ISSN 0379-3680 ƒ 25.00

Supersedes the "FID Yearbook" which was published through 1977 as FID 526.

*****

CURRENT ISSUES AND TRENDS IN EDUCATION AND TRAINING FOR INFORMATION WORK IN DEVELOPING COUNTRIES
The Hague, FID, 1981, viii, 193 p., (FID 595) ISBN 92-66-00595-9 ƒ 62.50

Contains the papers presented at the FID Education and Training Committee Workshop held in Copenhagen, Denmark, on 13-15 August 1980.

*****

GUIDE TO AGRICULTURAL INFORMATION SOURCES IN ASIA AND OCEANIA, edited by G.R.T. Levick for FID/CAO/AG
The Hague, FID, 1980, vi, 72 p., (FID 592) ISBN 92-66-00592-4 ƒ 40.00

Brief description of secondary sources — bibliographies and directories — of relevance to agricultural topics, with special reference to the Asia and Oceania Region

*****

CRITERIA OF THE QUALITY OF INFORMATION SYSTEMS AND PROCESSES
Moscow, VINITI, 1981, 182 p., (FID 591) (Theoretical Problems of Informatics 7) ISSN 0203-6495 ƒ 40.00

Contains 9 papers devoted to effectiveness of information systems.

*****

EDUCATION AND TRAINING FOR INFORMATION SERVICES IN BUSINESS AND INDUSTRY IN DEVELOPING AND DEVELOPED COUNTRIES: THE NEEDS, THE EXPERIENCE, THE NEWER TRENDS
The Hague, FID, 1980, v, 122 p., (FID 584) ISBN 92-66-00584-3 ƒ 55.00

Papers presented at the FID Education and Training Committee Workshop, Minneapolis, Minnesota, October 1979.

*****

INTERNATIONAL GUIDE TO FILMS ON INFORMATION SOURCES, 3rd edition
The Hague, FID, 1979, iv, 36 p. (FID 577) ISBN 92-66-00577-0 ƒ 18.00

Guide to 103 films, film strips, slide/tape presentations and videocassettes.

*****

INTERNATIONAL FEDERATION FOR DOCUMENTATION
P.O. BOX 30115
2500 GC The Hague, Netherlands

A complete list of imprint FID publications is available on request

31-07-1981

THREE TECHNICAL REPORT PRINTED INDEXES: A COMPARATIVE STUDY

Susan Copeland

I. Introduction

Libraries containing hundreds of thousands of technical reports are scattered throughout the United States, many with depository collections of reports from major government agencies such as the National Aeronautics and Space Administration (NASA) and the Department of Energy (DOE). In most of these libraries, routine access involves use of one or more of five printed indexes and the NTIS data base. While multiple studies have been published on the usefulness of online resources that provide access to technical reports, relatively little has been written comparing and evaluating the printed indexes. This is unfortunate, since many libraries have not yet incorporated on-the-spot online searching into their reference process, nor will they necessarily ever have the means to do so. In addition, libraries lacking extensive technical report collections often purchase some or all of the indexes, only to discover that they are used so rarely that librarians forget how, or when, to use them. As a result, technical report collections are generally a neglected and under-used resource, and librarians are purchasing indexes that may not be needed.

This study attempts to provide some basis of comparison for three major technical report indexes; *Government Reports Announcements and Index* (GRA&I), *Energy Research Abstracts* (ERA) and *Scientific and Technical Aerospace Reports* (STAR). While duplication in coverage and alphanumeric listings of report numbers are the primary topics of discussion, attention is given to the availability of report series listed in the indexes, the subject areas each index covers, and other types of materials within the indexes, such as patent listings and periodical references. Although this is a comparative study, it is not the intention of the author to make judgments as to the relative values of the indexes. That is the reader's prerogative.

II. The Approach

Anyone dealing with technical report indexes cannot help but notice an interrelationship among them, the most obvious being references in one index to abstracts found in another. The question of overlap there-

---

Susan Copeland is Bibliographer for Biology and Chemistry at Boston University. She received the BA degree from Capital University and the MS degree in Library Science from Columbia University.

fore seemed to be a valid one, and was the initial prompting that grew into this study.

Having found no previous research that might supply an answer, the next step was to define the limits of the study. Initially a project that would include all sources containing technical reports was considered, but speedily abandoned upon further investigation which revealed the quantity of sources potentially involved. Another option was to include data bases available online in the comparison. Ultimately the decision was made to focus on three primary printed technical report indexes, rather than attempt to cover the entire spectrum of technical report resources. It was hoped at that time that the limitation would make the study of more manageable proportions.

Choosing a sampling method that would best represent the material posed a new difficulty. Literally hundreds of different report series are covered by technical report indexes, many unique to a particular source. The sampling method had to list as many of those series as possible, while maintaining the realistic proportions within and among the series. Under these conditions, the best representative sample seemed to be an entire, single issue from each source.

The first issue of 1979 in each of the three indexes became the primary basis of comparison. However, comparing the first issues alone of the indexes would not produce significant results, since few sources index the same materials concurrently. Consequently, three separate sets of data were recorded, each composed of comparative statistics of entries that appeared either in the previous (1978) or subsequent (1979) annual indexes of each of the remaining sources. To chart the time lag, that is, the length of time required for each index to list the same information, the issue in which each report number appeared was noted and recorded. By using the report number indexes in conjunction with the abstract entries it was possible to compare and contrast indexing techniques among the sources. Finally, by incorporating the abstract entries into the bulk of the study, entries other than those referring to technical reports—theses, books, dissertations, periodical articles, and patents—became quantifiable.

Because of these additional entries, a working definition of "technical report" had to be developed. For the purpose of this study, the definition of a report is any reference to an item available through NTIS (National Technical Information Service), DOE, NASA, or IAEA (International Atomic Energy Agency) that has also been assigned a report or accession number by one or more agencies. Many conference proceedings are therefore included, as well as a few patent entries that meet the above noted definition. This is in no way an attempt to define a literature genre; other definitions were simply too ambiguous for the needs of this project.

Similarly, although "report number" and "accession number" may seem to be used interchangeably, there is a distinction. "Accession number," for the purposes of this study, refers to a unique number assigned or acknowledged by the primary distributor of a document. In a GRA&I entry, for example, the accession number is always located in the lower left corner, and is the number used to order the document from NTIS. In ERA index entries the number is within parentheses when included; STAR always uses the "N" prefix, the year (two digits) and a five-digit number. In this paper, an accession number entry listed alphanumerically in the report number indexes is referred to as a "prime" entry.

As for the actual gathering of data and documentation, a system was developed for optimum efficiency through manual methods. Unfortunately a computer was not readily available for time-consuming and tedious processes of counting and collating; these, too were accomplished through manual methods.

III. The Results

A. What the Indexes Cover

Each of the sources included in this study was created to serve a specific purpose, including but not restricted to listing technical report literature. Of the three indexes, GRA&I most nearly falls under the category of "technical report index"; 88.2% of the entries in the sample issue, abstract section, or 1620 of 1836 total entries, were references to technical reports (as defined in section II of this paper). Identified commonly as a catalog of reports that can be purchased through NTIS, GRA&I claims to index materials from four sources; DOE, NASA, DOD (Department of Defense) and a variety of other agencies. It is not restricted to listing reports in a particular subject area or discipline. GRA&I covers a limited amount of material not available through NTIS; primary non-NTIS series which are included are the ED- and HRP- prefixed series, the former being documents available through ERIC (Educational Resources Information Center), and the latter referring to periodical articles and documents in the health fields. 80 of the entries in the January 5, 1979, issue were references to patents, 41 of which are available through NTIS.

GRA&I is published biweekly (26 issues/year), with annual cumulative indexes. Like STAR and ERA, it provides a variety of index access points, such as corporate author, personal author, subject, report number and contract number indexes. Abstracts are now provided for all entries when available, a recent change in policy. Previously, if a reference were abstracted in STAR or ERA, the GRA&I entry would refer the user to the appropriate source.

Unlike GRA&I, STAR claims to cover only aeronautics, space, and supporting disciplines, including in its coverage NASA-owned patents and patent applications, theses and dissertations, translations, and reports issued by other government agencies. Cumulative indexes are published semiannually and annually; STAR is issued on the 8th and 23rd of each month. An additional and unique service that STAR provides is a listing of "on-going research projects" in the beginning of each semimonthly issue.

While the other sources examined in this study contain a number of journal, book and/or conference references, STAR does not. *International Aerospace Abstracts* (IAA), sponsored by NASA but not examined in this study, covers such information.

Of the 996 abstract entries in the first 1979 issue of STAR, 14.9% were identified as references to theses or dissertations. The remainder of the entries (848) fall under the definition of a technical report as it is used in this study, although included in this case in the designation are patents and translations. 56.6% of the 996 entries are listed as being available through NTIS, and are not NASA publications; 28.5% are NASA publications, many of which are available through NTIS. In fact, of the technical report listings, only 2.5% are listed as not being available through NTIS. In other words, 82.5% of the total 996 entries can be obtained through NTIS.

ERA, the third and final source to be examined, provides abstracting and indexing coverage for all publications sponsored by DOE. It also indexes energy and nuclear information from domestic and international agencies. 24 semimonthly issues are available each year, as well as a semiannual and annual index.

There was a total of 2138 abstracts in the January 15, 1979, issue. It was found that 53.2% (1137) of the entries could be identified as technical report references (of which 64.6%—735—were available through NTIS). As for the remainder of the 2138 entries, 41.8% (894) of the items were references to periodical articles, 4.5% (96) referred to patents, 0.5% (10) cited books, and only 1 entry referred to a thesis.

B. *Indexing Variations.*

As mentioned earlier, all three sources contain five indexes in addition to abstracts—subject, personal author, corporate author, contract number and accession number indexes. Each source provides a different degree of access within its indexes, as illustrated in Figure 1.

Since the report number indexes, in conjunction with the abstract entries, were used to determine the degree of overlap in coverage and the time lag, they will be discussed in somewhat greater detail.

In its report number index, GRA&I provides nearly complete bibliographic information

    AD-A058 983/8GI

    Spacecraft Charging at Geosynchronous Orbit
    Solution for Eclipse Passage.
    AD-A058 983/8GI   22A   PC A02/MF A01

in contrast to ERA

    AD-A-

      058983   4:47580   NTIS PCA02/MF A01

and STAR.

    AD-A058983 . . . . 03 p0290 N79-12132 #

FIGURE 1

INDEX CONTENTS

		AUTHOR	CORPORATE AUTHOR	REPORT #	CONTRACT #	TITLE	ABSTRACT CODE	AVAILABILITY	PRICE
STAR	AUTHOR	/					X		
	CORPORATE AUTHOR		/	X		X	X		
	REPORT #			/		X	X		
	CONTRACT #				/		X		
	SUBJECT			X		X	X		
ERA	AUTHOR	/		X		X	X		
	CORPORATE AUTHOR		/	X		X	X		
	REPORT #			/		X	X	X	
	CONTRACT #		X	X	/		X		
	SUBJECT			X		X	X		
GRA&I	AUTHOR	/		X		X	X	X *	X
	CORPORATE AUTHOR		/	X		X	X	X *	X
	REPORT #			/		X	X	X *	X
	CONTRACT #		X	X	/		X	X *	X
	SUBJECT			X		X	X	X *	X

* Availability information is simply a price code if available NTIS, or a message that the report is not available NTIS.

All the entries use a different method of referring the user to the appropriate abstract. GRA&I uses a category, or subject, code (in this case, 22A) and the accession number to arrange the abstract entries. ERA uses the volume number and an abstract number (4:47580). STAR entries contain an issue, page and abstract number, each abstract number being unique to a particular report (N79-12132).

STAR's system posed a problem for this study in that the abstract number is also, in many cases, the accession number for NASA technical reports. STAR signals this by adding an asterisk (*) after NASA-generated materials, and both an asterisk and a hash mark (#) after those entries that are both NASA-produced and available on microfiche. However, "N" prefixed accession numbers are not listed in STAR report number indexes alphanumerically, since every entry is assigned such a number, technical report or no. It was therefore necessary when comparing GRA&I and ERA to STAR to cross-reference all the "N" accession numbers appearing in the two sources using the abstracts.

ERA was the only source to use "see" references in its report number indexing; that is, the report number and abstract number would be listed, but the user then needed to check either the abstract or an additional report number entry for the report's availability and price. However, 38, or 5.4% of the report numbers listed in ERA were also listed in GRA&I under a different number, although no "see" reference was given in ERA. In most cases, the omitted listing was an NTIS accession number (PB- or AD-A-), a number probably later assigned by NTIS when GRA&I received the report. Similarly, 33.6% of the entries in GRA&I eventually identified in STAR were not listed in STAR under the "N" accession number given in GRA&I, but an alternate number.

The report number indexes vary not only in the levels of access they provide, but also in the variety of alphanumeric sequences each uses. While report numbers have been standardized to a great extent, certain small variations—the use of a slash instead of a dash, for example—still exist, and can cause problems both for the indexer in listing the numbers, and for the user in finding them within the report number indexes. To further illustrate, let us examine the following sequence of numbers:

    ANL-AMD-TM-262
    ANL-CT-77-3
    ANL-76-XX-73
    ANL-77-XX-37
    ANL-77-14
    ANL-8000-REV-2
    ANL/CEN/FE-77-2
    CONF 770941-1
    CONF 771015-5
    CONF 7709120-1
    CONF 7710101-3

These numbers are listed as they appear in STAR. From this listing, one might make some broad generalizations concerning alphanumeric ordering, such as: (1) dashes precede slashes; (2) letters precede numbers; (3) years precede other numbers; and (4) numbers (excluding years) are filed as whole numbers.

ERA, on the other hand, uses an entirely different system. In this source, report numbers containing dashes and slashes are interfiled;

numbers precede letters, and while three and four digit numbers are filed as whole numbers, the larger six and seven digit numbers are not. In fact, each series seems to be handled differently depending upon the nature of the series. The same sequence above would be listed in ERA like this:

ANL-76-XX-73
ANL-77-14
ANL-77-XX-37
ANL-8000-(Rev. 2)
ANL-AMD-TM—262
ANL/CEN/FE-77-2
ANL-CT-77-3
CONF 770941-1
CONF 7709120-1
CONF 771015-5
CONF 7710101-3

Another difference in the indexing in ERA is the use of lower case letters (note the fourth entry in the example above). STAR uses no lower case letters in its report number indexing.

GRA&I uses yet another variation on the basic alphanumeric system:

ANL-AMD-TM-262
ANL/CEN/FE-77-2
ANL-CT-77-3
ANL-76-XX-73
ANL-77-XX-37
ANL-77-14
ANL-8000 (REV. 2)
CONF 770941-1
CONF 771015-5
CONF 7709120-1
CONF 7710101-3

Other variations noted in GRA&I were the occasional use of lower case letters (ORNL-tr-1034, e.g.) and variations in the report numbers themselves, such as omitting "REV. 2" from the example above, or adding "VOL. 1 PT. 1" to a report number when appropriate. In each case the report itself was determined to be identical to the listing in one or more of the other indexes, although the identifying numbers differed slightly.

Due to the nature of report number indexes, multiple listings are common for a single report. In addition, STAR and ERA may abstract a single large report in several separate sections, assigning different abstract numbers (but the same accession number) to each entry.

ERA was the only index examined during this study discovered to have a serious indexing flaw. Volume 4 (1979) issues 20 and 23 were distributed containing author indexing through "B" only. These issues were replaced by the agency at later date, fully corrected.

C. Overlap.

There was, as expected, a high degree of duplicate indexing among the sources. 94.3% of the report entries in STAR were at some time included in GRA&I; GRA&I picked up 78.8% of the technical report entries in ERA. Conversely, only 40.6% of the material in GRA&I's technical report index also appeared in STAR, while 20.8% was covered by ERA.

These numbers should be considered in relation to both the natures of the sources and their relative sizes. In the January 5, 1979, issue of GRA&I there were 3,372 report number index entries, 1,836 being prime entries. The STAR issue for the same period contained a total of 1,153 entries, and ERA contained 1,163 technical report references in its index. Combined, STAR and ERA covered only 44.6% of the technical report entries listed in GRA&I.

The question of time lag, or the amount of time a source takes to cover the same information listed in another source, is most efficiently and effectively represented by charts.

Figures 2 and 3 show the number of technical report references in GRA&I (January 5, 1979) that were picked up by STAR and ERA, respectively, and indicate in which issues they appeared.

33.3% of the material indexed also by STAR appeared first in STAR,

FIGURE 2

BREAKDOWN OF STAR ISSUES COVERING GRA&I ISSUE 1/5/79

STAR ISSUE	NO. OF ENTRIES	PERCENTAGE
78/12	2	.1
78/17	1	.1
78/20	1	.1
78/22	19	1.4
78/23	427	31.2
78/24	6	.4
79/01	2	.1
79/02	5	.4
79/03	112	8.2
79/04	319	23.3
79/05	115	8.4
79/06	339	24.8
79/07	19	1.4
79/10	1	.1

TOTAL IN GRA&I   3,372

TOTAL ALSO IN STAR   1,368

FIGURE 3

BREAKDOWN OF ERA ISSUES COVERING GRA&I ISSUE 1/5/79

ERA ISSUE	NO. OF ENTRIES	PERCENTAGE
78/01	1	.1
78/03	2	.3
78/05	2	.3
78/09	2	.3
78/12	1	.1
78/16	1	.1
78/19	14	2.0
78/20	2	.3
78/21	55	7.9
78/22	362	51.7
78/23	1	.1
78/24	3	.5
79/01	9	1.3
79/02	15	2.1
79/03	4	.6
79/04	6	.9
79/05	8	1.1
79/06	29	4.1
79/07	8	1.1
79/08	3	.5
79/09	8	1.1
79/10	11	1.6
79/11	4	.6
79/18	148	21.2
79/23	1	.1

TOTAL IN GRA&I 3,372

TOTAL ALSO IN STAR 700

48.1% of the material was indexed within three months of its appearance in GRA&I, and only two entries appeared concurrently. A total of 1,368 entries were also indexed by STAR, an overlap of 40.6%.

In Figure 3, 56.7% of the material appeared first in ERA, with 20.9% indexed exactly 9½ months later than the January 5 issue of GRA&I. 700 entries were duplicated in ERA, or 20.8%.

FIGURE 4

BREAKDOWN OF GRA&I ISSUES COVERING STAR ISSUE 1/8/79

GRA&I ISSUE	NO. OF ENTRIES	PERCENTAGE
(74 - 78)	130	12.0
78/06	3	.3
78/07	5	.5
78/08	2	.2
78/10	3	.3
78/12	22	2.0
78/13	19	1.7
78/14	8	.7
78/15	2	.2
78/18	60	5.5
78/19	10	.9
78/20	122	11.2
78/21	189	17.4
78/22	213	19.5
78/23	34	3.1
78/24	3	.3
78/25	19	1.7
78/26	15	1.4
79/01	1	.1
79/02	4	.4
79/03	189	17.4
79/04	23	2.1
79/06	4	.4
79/10	3	.3
79/11	1	.1
79/13	3	.3

TOTAL IN STAR 1,153

TOTAL ALSO IN GRA&I 1087

Figures 4 and 5 illustrate report references in STAR that are also in GRA&I and ERA. 1,087 of 1,153 entries in STAR appeared in GRA&I, for a total overlap of 94.3%. Note, however, that 130, or 12% of the entries, appeared in GRA&I several years before they appeared in

STAR. These entries are "NTIS/PS-" series reports, accession numbers for published computer searches produced by NTIS.

195 of 1,153 entries in STAR were in ERA, a 16.9% coverage duplicaton.

Finally, figures 6 and 7 provide statistics for technical report entries in ERA that have also appeared in STAR and GRA&I.

The figures indicate that 81 of the 1,163 entries in the sample issue of

FIGURE 5

BREAKDOWN OF ERA ISSUES COVERING STAR ISSUE 1/8/79

ERA ISSUE	NO. OF ENTRIES	PERCENTAGE
78/01	5	2.6
78/02	5	2.6
78/03	6	3.1
78/04	1	.5
78/06	4	2.1
78/07	23	11.8
78/08	21	10.8
78/09	6	3.1
78/12	1	.5
78/16	1	.5
78/17	2	1.0
78/18	17	8.7
78/19	35	17.9
78/20	7	3.6
78/24	1	.5
79/01	4	2.1
79/02	1	.5
79/03	1	.5
79/05	2	1.0
79/07	2	1.0
79/08	25	12.8
79/09	7	3.6
79/10	17	8.7
79/12	1	.5

TOTAL IN STAR 1,153

TOTAL ALSO IN ERA 195

ERA were carried in STAR, or 7%; 917 of the 1,163 entries were in GRA&I, a duplicaton of 78.8%.

IV. Conclusion

There are many other resources that contain technical report references that were not included in this study. The Superintendent of Documents' *Monthly Catalog* routinely indexes those technical reports which are available through them, as well as some scattered NTIS reports. The *INIS Atomindex* also was not covered, although it is a major source of IAEA documents and reports from the Department of Energy.

The major focus of this study was not technical reports per se, but three major technical report indexes—their overlap, structure, and

FIGURE 6

BREAKDOWN OF STAR ISSUES COVERING ERA ISSUE 1/15/79

STAR ISSUE	NO. OF ENTRIES	PERCENTAGE
78/12	1	1.2
78/14	3	3.8
78/15	9	11.1
78/17	2	2.5
78/20	4	5.9
78/24	2	2.5
79/01	5	6.2
79/02	4	5.9
79/03	1	1.2
79/04	1	1.2
79/06	1	1.2
79/10	1	1.2
79/18	3	3.8
79/21	24	29.6
79/22	18	22.2
79/23	2	2.5

TOTAL IN ERA 1,163

TOTAL ALSO IN STAR 81

FIGURE 7

BREAKDOWN OF GRA&I ISSUES COVERING ERA ISSUE 1/15/79

GRA&I ISSUE	NO. OF ENTRIES	PERCENTAGE
78/23	1	.1
78/22	2	.2
78/21	6	.7
78/20	2	.2
78/19	7	.7
78/18	5	.5
78/16	4	.4
78/14	1	.1
78/12	19	2.1
78/10	1	.1
78/09	1	.1
79/01	6	.7
79/02	2	.2
79/03	3	.3
79/04	33	3.6
79/05	95	21.3
79/06	517	67.3
79/07	4	.4
79/09	1	.1
79/10	4	.4
79/11	1	.1
79/12	2	.2

TOTAL IN ERA 1,163

TOTAL ALSO IN GRA&I 917

coverage. In addition, report number indexes were carefully examined and compared to allow the reader to use them more confidently. This was not a "critical" study; no source, in the opinion of this author, came out a "winner" or was particularly shamed by the "competition." As librarians faced with the facts of tightened budgets and a broadening network of interlibrary cooperation, however, we have a responsibility to our users and our budgets to know what we are buying.

MANAGING EXXON'S TECHNICAL REPORTS

Karen Landsberg
Ben H. Weil

ABSTRACT. The technical information contained in Exxon reports is managed by use of an in-house, computerized system that builds a database and produces current-awareness "Report Alerts," various indexes including a subject KWIC, an online database, and reports-distribution control. Key elements in the system are: (1) a structural report number that incorporates codes for the issuing unit, major subject, and date; (2) natural-language indexing sentences that make up a pseudo abstract; and (3) controlled subject categories that are a base for the "Reports Alerts" system.

The technical reports of Exxon Research and Engineering Company and its affiliates are the formal records of their research and engineering studies. As such, they have long received careful management. This is currently the responsibility of the Company's Analytical and Information Division (AID), which collects, indexes, microfilms, and provides secondary distribution of the reports under systems designed to transfer their information to scientists and engineers who need it. In this work, AID utilizes modern information technologies to ensure the accessibility and security of this information.

History

Accessing of the information in Exxon Corporation's[1] technical reports was one of the early functions of Exxon Research's Research Library in Linden, NJ. The Library itself began functioning in 1920, during the first year of Exxon's organized research effort. Almost immediately, it began publishing bulletins of literature and patent abstracts, preparing literature searches and technical translations, and doing other work typical of a broad-based, technical, special library. In 1938 the Library produced a cumulative subject index to 1928-1937 Exxon reports and began a series of annual "Technical Report Indexes" that has been continued with considerable elaboration to this day.

Concurrently, the Library began collecting and maintaining a master set of the refining-related reports issued in the Exxon network, and preparing a microform record of these reports for use by other Exxon report centers. These basic collections, of course, made possible the

---

Karen Landsberg is at present in charge of Information Systems in Exxon Research and Engineering Company's Linden Information Center at the Analytical and Information Division, Exxon Research and Engineering Company, PO Box 121, Linden, NJ 07036. She has a B.S. in Chemistry from Drexel University and a M.S. in Physical Chemistry from Rutgers.

Ben H. Weil is a Senior Staff Advisor in the Analytical and Information Division of Exxon Research and Engineering Company. He holds B.S. and M.S. degrees in chemical engineering, and has managed technical-information operations at four organizations prior to his present staff assignment.

central report-indexing program. Exxon-affiliate cooperation in sending in copies of their reports, as issued, is part of their implementation of their research agreements with Exxon Research. A Library-associated group was also established as the clearance center for "reports-distribution control"—arrangements for people in the affiliates to receive on a regular basis the Exxon reports to which they are entitled by agreement, and for provision of (or clearance for receipt of) copies of specific other reports that they request. While this paper will be focused on the indexing and retrieval programs, it is important to realize here that they are parts of a relatively complete reports-management program.

The subject portions of early technical-report indexes were of the conventional, alphabetical-index type. By the 1950's, however, more sophisticated, "alphabetical-classed" indexing ws employed. At the end of that decade, attention began to be given to the development of a controlled-language, coordinate-indexing system, then a pioneering idea. The precepts and details of such a system were subsequently tested in a pilot program on Exxon Research's engineering reports and memoranda. More importantly, they were the basis for team work (1961-1963) on the development of the thesaurus-based indexing system of the American Petroleum Institute's Central Abstracting and Indexing Service (API-CAIS).

Before this system could be employed for Exxon report indexing, however, several developments intervened. The Exxon technical-report indexes had traditionally been produced on an annual basis, covering reports issued in each calendar year, but the alphabetical-classed indexing required for each annual index had begun to take 1.5 years to complete, even with an increase in staff. By 1962, issuance of indexes had fallen nearly two years behind, and it became evident that we could not await the completion of the controlled-language system.

Fortuitously, however, one of us had become aware of the KWIC (Key-Word-In-Context) system developed by Bell Laboratories[2] to index the titles of its correspondence, publications, and pertinent outside literature. Through the courtesy of Bell, the computer program for this system was made available to us. Also with Bell's help, we modified this program to permit permuting (rotating) multiple indexing sentences[3] for each report, one at a time, instead of rotating only the words in the title. This permitted us to do relatively deep (but natural-language) report indexing, and by 1963 we had caught up by issuing KWIC sentence indexes for our 1961 and 1962 reports. Pro tem, we labeled these "interim indexes," because we still planned to re-index the reports under the API-CAIS system, but we were also benefitting from the currency of our indexing by being able to issue "Monthly Technical Report Indexes" as an alerting for researchers, something that had never before been possible.

In 1964 our Linden Information Center began to use the API-CAIS' controlled-language system to index the bulletins of literature and patent abstracts that we ourselves were preparing, the purpose being to augment the API-CAIS' abstracting/indexing efforts. By 1965 we had learned that the level of effort required for this type of indexing was a sizable multiple of that required for multiple-sentence KWIC indexing; unfortunately, indeed, we were now well behind in our controlled-language indexing of these abstracts. Concurrently, we had also become pleasantly aware that our "interim" multiple-sentence KWIC indexes for technical reports were serving far better than had ever been imagined—better, apparently, than had the alphabetical-classed indexes.

One and one added up to two. We continued to prepare multiple-sentence (deep) KWIC indexes for Exxon technical reports, and we shifted to augmented-title KWIC indexing for literature and patents for as long as this program continued. In 1970, we began a similar augmented title program for correspondence. Our present programs are derivatives—technological updates—of these happenings.

We do not contend that natural-language indexing such as ours can conveniently provide everything that is possible with controlled-language systems, for example, ready generic-specific and chemical-substructure access. However, modern information technology is rapidly easing such problems, and the advantages of using natural language are many. After all, the all-important "links" and "role indicators" needed in controlled-language descriptor indexing are simply attempts to restore attributes of natural "full text."

One last aspect of our reports-accessing history merits some attention. Although, as mentioned, the Library had long prepared abstracts of the literature and patents for publication in in-house current-awareness bulletins and for retrieval from subject-classified card files, the Library had never prepared similar abstracts for Exxon technical reports. By the mid-1960's, however, we realized that the set of KWIC sentences being prepared for each report amounted to a pseudo abstract, and we began to use these sets as such for a variety of purposes.

These pseudo abstracts became particularly important in the late 1960's and early 1970's when, for several years, we loaded the keywords from each report-index sentence into a batch computer-searching system that had been designed originally for use with controlled-language terms. To avoid wasting time with errors caused by Boolean combination of terms from discrete sentences, it became highly desirable to compensate for false drops by looking at the corresponding pseudo abstracts before going to the full reports. Today, these pseudo abstracts form the base for our interactive online retrieval system and are used on our Report Alerts, as described later.

Reports Handling

Approximately 2,000 technical reports are produced annually by more than 100 Exxon affiliates in the areas for which we provide access—petroleum refining and products, synthetic fuels, engineering, chemicals, corporate research, etc.. In the main, these are formal reports of investigations, but we also index consultants' reports, substantive progress reports, and other proprietary documents that contain technical information that may not be reported more formally later. By arrangement, we receive at least two copies of each Exxon technical report. One of these is promptly sent to our Micrographic Center, which prepares standard (98-frame) negative microfiche of all such reports and distributes weekly sets of these microfiche to Exxon-affiliate report centers, in time to backup the "Report Alerts" that are sent to Exxon staffs, and for later retrieval by these affiliate centers and by our own reports center.[4] The other report copy is used for indexing and then for archival storage as part of our records-retention program.

The actual technical indexing will be discussed later. At various times and by various indexers it has been done by writing the indexing sentences in longhand, by dictating and stenographic transcribing, or by direct writing on minicomputer-input terminals. Bibliographic information from the reports is input by clerks into minicomputer terminals.

As also mentioned earlier, Exxon Research's Analytical and Information Division is also responsible for implementing Exxon Research's research agreements with affiliates by arranging for the correct distribution of contract-entitled reports and, more dynamically, for assuring optimum distribution. Computer correlations of data on contract entitlements, report series, and standardized addresses of report issuers and individual recipients allow us to prepare updated lists of authorized recipients, which are periodically sent to report issuers. Sets of sticky-back mailing labels are also regularly supplied or are available on demand. Exxon Research's Law Department is, of course, responsible for contract development and compliance, but AID's efforts implement these.

Computer System

Exxon's technical-report system at present utilizes a computerized in-house Information Management Program. The program is versatile and is used for many purposes by various Exxon affiliates; it builds databases using minicomputers for data entry input. Friendly screens with fixed fields have been developed to expedite the data entry. The input information is then transmitted to a mainframe computer for processing and for batch generation of reports and other information products.

Reports Database Unit Record

The computer system uses a general indexing program, and data are entered to create a unit record for each report. The unit report record contains both bibliographic and subject information; a sample is shown in Figure 1.

Bibliographic Information

A cornerstone of the reporting system is the unique number that is given to each report. This report number identifies not only the report, but also the group doing the work, the subject area, and the year of issue. It has the following form:

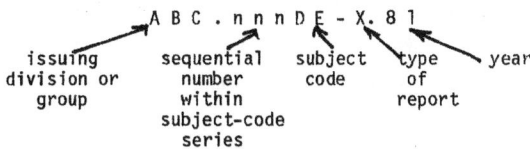

```
         A B C . n n n D E - X. 8 1
      issuing    sequential    subject    type      year
     division or   number       code      of
       group       within                report
                 subject-code
                   series
```

The first portion of the report number is the issuing-unit code, which identifies the Exxon group or division reporting the work. Over 100 Exxon groups, worldwide, participate in this report-numbering system, which we coordinate; each has its unique issuing-unit code.

The alphabetic section of the middle portion of the report number usually indicates the main subject area of the report. Over 120 broad subject categories, designated by two-letter codes, are presently employed. The numerical part of the middle portion indicates the sequential number of the report for that year within the issuing unit's specific-subject series. Optional characters at the end of the middle portion (following a hyphen) designate the type of report, e.g., progress (-P), highlight (-H), review (-R), etc.

The third portion of the report number consists of the last two digits of the year in which the report was issued. Exxon report numbers are assigned or logged in by local information centers.

The Exxon report numbers contain all of the elements and most of the

Figure 1. Unit Report Record.

Report Number   - CR.1180.80

Title   - A Comprehensive Study of the Thermodynamic Properties of
                      Perdeuterated Cyclohexane (Cyclohexane-d_{12}) - 30 pgs.

Authors   - S. C. Mraw and D. F. Naas - O'Rourke

Corporate Author   - ER&E - Corporate Research

Subject Categories - BO - Physical Chemistry
                      BA - Analysis and Testing
                      GA - Coal Characterization

Subject Sentences   -   Low-temperature heat capacity and enthalpies of
                      solid-solid phase transition and fusion of
                      cyclohexane-d_{12} determined by differential scanning
                      calorimetry.
                          The entropy of ideal gaseous cyclohexane-d_{12}
                      calculated from spectroscopic data.
                          Thermodynamic properties of perdeuterated
                      cyclohexane determined from laboratory and literature
                      data.
                          Thermodynamic properties of cyclohexane-d_{12}
                      determined for studied of solvent absorption in coal
                      pores.

Figure 2. Petroleum-Product Subject Categories and Codes.

```
P-  - Petroleum Products, General
    PA  - Gas and Oil Production
    PB  - Fuels
        PC  - Motor Gasolines
        PD  - Middle Distillates
        PE  - Aviation Fuels
        PF  - Residual Fuels
    . . . . . . . . . . . . . . .
    PO  - Gases
        PR  - Liquified Natural Gas
        PP  - Liquified Petroleum Gas, etc.
```

other specifications of the ANSI Standard Technical Report Number (STRN). One of us was a member of the ANSI-Z39 Subcommittee that formulated this standard (ANSI Z39.23-1974).

The original title of the report is usually used in its unit record; however, it is amplified when needed. The number of pages in the report is also indicated in the title field. When appropriate, the report date is included, since for a series of reports, especially progress reports, this can also be significant.

All of the authors are included in the citation. They are, of course, individually searchable in the database. The authors' affiliation, division, or group is also included in the unit record.

Subject Categories

As indicated above, the Exxon report system presently employs over 120 broad subject categories. These are the controlled terms of the technical-reports database. The various subject categories reflect the diverse research interests of Exxon and its affiliates. Major classifications include petroleum processes, petroleum products, additives, basic research, chemicals, engineering, etc. When possible, codes are grouped in hierarchical series as illustrated in Figure 2. The system is dynamic, and changes are made as needed to accommodate new activities and projects.

The middle portion of the report number can indicate the major subject category or classification of the document and is determined by the issuing unit. However, a report may be assigned up to ten additional subject codes by the indexer to cover fully both its contents and its applications. The subject categories are multipurpose. Specific categories are used to generate targeted current-awareness announcements (SDI-type reports called "Report Alerts"). The subject codes are also used to produce customized report indexes. Lastly, they can be used as parameters for controlled subject retrieval in online searching.

Natural-Language Indexing

Each report is indexed by writing a pseudo abstract of what we term individual "sentences"; 5 to 7 sentences are usually required. (See Figure 1.) Natural language is employed, consisting of the author(s)' terminology and appropriate additional terms. These sentences are multifunctional and define the content and scope of the report. Combined, the sentences must also constitute a readable abstract for use in a current-awareness report and for the online-database citation. Individually, each sentence must be complete enough for use in a KWIC permuted subject index (described later). Finally, the individual terms in each sentence must be useful as natural-language keywords in online subject searching using Boolean operators.

The pseudo abstract is reader-oriented. Whenever practical, it summarizes what was done rather than simply listing the chemicals, products, techniques, and instruments involved. It attempts to provide an explanation of why the work was done. Although chemical formulas, abbreviations, and acronyms are used, they are always defined in one of the KWIC sentences of the citation. This makes possible identification or recall of a report by a variety of approaches.

The computer program written for reports indexing imposes certain constraints on the text field; our own practices impose others. The KWIC sentences that we employ have a maximum length of 120 characters, including the report-number field. Ideally, the length of the text in each individual line falls within the imposed limit. When this limit is exceeded, the computer provides beginning or end truncation, depending on the location of the key term in the alphabetic array. Some of the system's reports indexes and Alerts also display a maximum of only 26

Figure 3. Report Alert

REPORT ALERT
PROPRIETARY INFORMATION

REPORT NUMBER: CR.21BD.80

NEW REPORT ON: CATALYSIS, SURFACE PHYSICS, INORGANIC CHEMISTRY

TITLE: CATALYTIC HYDROGENATION OF GRAPHITE BY PLATINUM, IRIDIUM, AND PLATINUM-IRIDIUM - 22 PGS.

AUTHOR: BAKER, RTK; SHERWOOD, RD; DUMESIC, JA OF ER&E CORPORATE RESEARCH

KEY TOPICS: DISPERSION AND REDISPERSION OF PLATINUM AND IRIDIUM PARTICLES SUPPORTED ON GRAPHITE.
SURFACE EFFECTS OF HEATING PT-IR CATALYST PARTICLES IN HYDROGEN.
SURFACE BEHAVIOR OF BIMETALLIC PARTICLES IN A REDUCING ENVIRONMENT DURING CATALYTIC HYDROGENATION OF GRAPHITE.

lines of text. However, we have found that the great majority of our reports can be well handled and indexed within these constraints.

Products

The database for the Exxon reports system provides three major products—current awareness announcements, cumulative indexes, and an online interactive capability.

The Report Alerts (targeted, current-awareness announcements) are computer-produced weekly for all the reports indexed that week and are distributed worldwide to Exxon scientists and engineers; a sample is shown in Figure 3. We have used Report Alerts as a current-awareness tool since 1974. Reports are indexed within one to two weeks after we receive them at our information center, so the Alerts are an effective and efficient current-awareness product. Last year, we sent out over 400,000 individual Report Alerts. When new recipients begin to use this alerting system, they indicate which of the subject categories are of interest to them; they then receive Report Alerts for all reports that were coded with those selected subject categories. Copies of the full reports that are deemed to be of interest are then obtained by Report-Alert users from their local Exxon report centers.

For each year, cumulative computer-output microfiche (COM) indexes for subjects, authors, and report numbers (Figure 4) are produced monthly and distributed to the Exxon report centers. Multi-year cumulative indexes are also generated and distributed as needed. The subject (KWIC) index contains individually rotated sentences and also the report's title. This KWIC index thereby highlights every meaningful word in the report citation (Figure 4). Alphabetic author and alphanumeric report number listings are also produced. The sequence of the report numbers in this latter listing provides easy identification of either a single report or a sequential subject series of a division's reports. The actual reports are also filed in this order in both our hard-copy and microform collections.

Although the Exxon report centers receive the complete "Technical Reports Index" (our long-time name for these indexes), we have also found it useful to provide customized cuts of the reports database to various refineries and other groups. Thus, for example, an index of those reports most useful to refinery operations is generated and sent to various Exxon refineries worldwide. Special report indexes appropriate to the needs of other groups, such as Plastics and Olefins, are also produced and distributed.

Exxon has various other proprietary databases. We also produce some additional targeted indexes that reference several types of relevant documents, such as Exxon publications, reports, and correspondence, by merging appropriate databases.

Online Databases

One of the important features of the Exxon technical-report system is an online interactive reports database. Exxon uses a modern, versatile software system that provides all of the advantages presently afforded by publicly available online interactive systems—speed, flexibility,

Figure 4. Report Indexes

NUMBER INDEX

CR.21BD.80   CATALYTIC HYDROGENATION OF GRAPHITE BY PLATINUM, IRIDIUM AND PLATINUM-IRIDIUM - 22PGS.

              BAKER, RTK; SHERWOOD, RD; DUMESIC, JA

              DISPERSION AND REDISPERSION OF PLATINUM AND IRIDIUM PARTICLES
              SUPPORTED ON GRAPHITE.

              SURFACE EFFECTS OF HEATING PT-IR CATALYST PARTICLES IN
              HYDROGEN.

              SURFACE BEHAVIOR OF BIMETALLIC PARTICLES IN A REDUCING ENVIRON-
              MENT DURING CATALYTIC HYDROGENATION OF GRAPHITE.

SUBJECT (KWIC) INDEX

CATALYTIC HYDROGENATION OF GRAPHITE BY PLATINUM   IRIDIUM AND PLATINUM-IRIDIUM   CR.21BD.80
         CATALYTIC OXIDATION OF GRAPHITE BY   IRIDIUM AND RHODIUM   CR.2BD.80
                    INHIBITION OF SINTERING OF   IRIDIUM/ALUMINA CATALYSTS   EL.4BD.80
              THE MECHANISM OF OXIDATION OF   IRON AND IRON-CHROMIUM ALLOYS IN DILUTE CHLORINE GAS   SR.7DG.80
                 MECHANISM OF CHLORINATION OF   IRON AT ELEVATED TEMPERATURES   SR.12DG.80
                   THERMO-MAGNETIC STUDIES OF   IRON COMPOUNDS IN COAL CHAR   EE.6GA.80

AUTHOR INDEX

BAKER, LE   SR.5BD.80   VAPOUR PHASE ADSORPTION MEASUREMENTS OF C6 HYDROCARBON MIXTURES ON SYNTHETIC FAUJASITE - 16 PGS.

BAKER, RTK   CR.8BV.80   CHEMISORPTION PROPERTIES OF IRIDIUM ON ALUMINA CATALYSTS - 4 PGS.
              CR.21BD.80   CATALYTIC HYDROGENATION OF GRAPHITE BY PLATINUM, IRIDIUM AND PLATINUM-IRIDIUM - 22 PPS.
              CR.6BD.80   CATALYTIC OXIDATION OF GRAPHITE BY IRIDIUM AND RHODIUM - 10 PGS.

BALDWIN, FP   ET.5CW.80   POLYOLEFIN ELASTOMERS BASED ON ETHYLENE AND PROPYLENE - 25 PGS.

Boolean operators, truncation, full text-searching, bibliometric analysis, etc. Thus, the online reports database not only ensures comprehensive subject and author retrieval, but also provides various statistics and other data when they are needed. Searchable fields include title, text (the index sentences), author, issuing division, subject categories, issue date (year), and type of report.

Staffing

Exxon presently has 1½ technical indexers involved with the technical-reports systems—chemists with Masters' degrees. The indexers have (or must develop) a broad technical background, because of the diversity of Exxon's interests. They write the textual sentences and assign the pertinent subject categories. A clerk inputs into the minicomputer system the indexing information provided by the technical indexers as well as the bibliographic information taken directly from the reports. Additional staff members film, file, distribute, and maintain the report collection.

Use

The technical-reports system is an invaluable Exxon resource. It is highly regarded and utilized. Our central information center alone responded to over 18,000 requests for secondarydistribution of technical reports last year. Local centers provided additional services. Most of the requests for reports come from readers of the Report Alerts; subsequent requests develop from conversations among researchers and engineers and from report searching.

Report searching is often done by individuals at various Exxon report centers from local sets of the COM-produced and cumulated technical report indexes. In addition to report center staff, many Exxon researchers browse the indexes for themselves before starting new projects; engineers often search it to find rapid answers to immediate problems. However, today we find that report searching is increasingly being done by using the online interactive reports database. Information-center staffs regularly search the reports database and indexes in order to answer technical questions.

The Exxon Technical Report System provides current awareness, retrieval, and a complete 50-year collection of reports. It provides rapid and comprehensive access to and retrieval of information on Exxon's research and technology. Although we are constantly looking for ways to improve this system, we are reasonably satisfied with the way that it continues to serve us.

REFERENCE NOTES

1. We are using only our present names here, and not such earlier actual ones as "Standard Oil Company (NJ)," "Standard Oil Development Company," and "Esso Research and Engineering Company."
2. Kennedy, R.A. Applications of permutation indexing. *Journal of Chemical Documentation.* 2(1): 181-185; 1962.
3. Called "synthetic titles" by Peter Luhn of IBM.
4. To make on-demand hard copies or duplicate microfiche.

LABORATORY NOTEBOOK STORAGE AND RETRIEVAL SYSTEMS

C. Margaret Bell

ABSTRACT: Despite the general conclusion that laboratory notebooks contain valuable and often needed data, there has been relatively little discussion in the literature on the development of an adequate storage and retrieval system for them. To determine the various possibilities of such a system, a survey of 83 food science libraries was conducted. 60% of the libraries employed some kind of a system. Four different systems were identified; and the system that allowed access by notebook author and notebook accession number was predominant.

Introduction

It has been recognized, not only in research laboratories but also in technical libraries, that an adequately prepared, well organized laboratory notebook should be available for future reference. If compiled in the manner described by Hughson[1], the laboratory notebook can be used as a detailed guide on laboratory procedures; to protect existing patents; to help propose new patents; to prevent reinvention; and to provide background information to new laboratory researchers.

However, no matter how accurate or authoritative a notebook is, it is worthless if the data cannot be easily and quickly retrieved. A study of record keeping practices conducted by BASF Wyandotte Corporation[2] discusses basic criteria for a feasible laboratory record system. The major criteria include cost effectiveness on the part of materials, user, and clerical costs; convenience; flexibility to include many different forms of data; good physical integrity; simplicity of filing and retrieval; and the ability to assist litigation.

Literature Survey

A search of the literature was performed and only three articles pertaining to laboratory notebook storage and retrieval (S&R) systems were located. Bailey[3] described a system that permitted access to information in notebooks by notebook number, notebook author, and general subjects. Upon return of a completed notebook to the library, the librarian records: 1) Notebook number; 2) Person(s) who used the notebook; 3) Subjects covered by the notebook; 4) Inclusive dates during which the work in the notebook was performed; and 5) Number of notebook pages

---

The author is currently Information Specialist at General Foods Technical Information Center, Library, 555 S. Broadway, Tarrytown, N.Y. 10591. She obtained her masters in library science from the State University of New York at Albany. She also obtained a B.S. in home economics and a minor in chemistry from St. Joseph College, West Hartford, Ct. The research in this paper was done when the author was a library school student at S.U.N.Y.

used. To retrieve these notebooks, index cards are prepared for each notebook, notebook author, and subjects covered in the notebook. These cards are filed numerically in a notebook number file and alphabetically in an author file and general subject file.

Mendenhall[4] described a system that involved computerized subject and author indexes to the notebooks. Scientists fill out standardized data cards to supplement the information in their completed lab notebook. The data includes notebook number, name of scientist, molecular formula, and other pertinent information. This information is used to generate subject and author indexes to the notebooks.

More recently, Cibbarelli et al.[5] described a computerized notebook S&R system called Libnotes, which is at present being employed at Allergan pharmaceuticals. With this system, each page of the notebook is scanned to identify seven predetermined retrieval elements: notebook number; persons(s) responsible for the notebook; department responsible for the notebook; inclusive years; in-house project numbers; in-house formulation numbers; and a controlled vocabulary substance index. These data elements are then entered into an in-house computer system and sorted on specific data elements to produce lists. Although these lists may contain all seven of the data elements, they are usually modified to provide only the substance terms and the corresponding notebook number. Access to lab notebooks could thus range from one to seven data elements with this Libnotes system.

Research Methodology

A survey of the United States food science libraries listed in the "Science and Technology Libraries" section of the *Subject Directory of Special Libraries and Information Centers*[6] was conducted. Of the 111 food science libraries listed, only those libraries that contained a collection of 900 or more items were selected. A questionnaire was sent to the 83 libraries that met these requirements. As shown in Figure 1, the questionnaire requested information on the various procedures involved with the individual library's notebook storage and retrieval system, including access points, cataloging, storage, and retrieval. In addition, any perceived drawbacks to the system were requested. The questionnaire concluded with a request for an updated description of the library.

Analysis of Results

Although the results of this questionnaire are directly applicable only to food science libraries, they can be generalized to other research and development libraries that keep laboratory notebooks.

Sixty of the 83 surveyed libraries responded, a 72% return. Table 1 shows the survey results. It was discovered that 17 of the 60 libraries surveyed do not handle laboratory notebooks at all. In an additional seven libraries, the individual departments in the institution performing the research kept the completed notebooks in the research laboratory or department office. The researchers in these departments usually employed their own storage and retrieval system. Usually the researchers

FIGURE 1: SAMPLE QUESTIONNAIRE

ADDRESS

DATE

ADDRESS OF SELECTED
FOOD SCIENCE LIBRARY

Dear

As a graduate library school student at S.U.N.Y. in Albany, I am currently doing research on the laboratory notebook storage and retrieval system in a research and development library. I was wondering if you could provide me with any information on your library's laboratory notebook system, if you do employ one.

To be more specific, can you describe the various procedures involved with the indexing (i.e. kinds of access points); cataloging; storage; and retrieval of the lab notebook? Do you feel that there are any drawbacks with your system? If so, can you describe them?

Lastly, is the below description of your library correct? If not, could you update it?

Photocopy of library's description found in
Subject Directory of Special Libraries.

Thank you very much for your time and cooperation.

Sincerely,

Margaret Bell

filed the notebooks according to subject matter and then chronologically within each subject. In this situation, the lab notebooks are not readily available to other researchers in the organization.

Thus, a total of 24 libraries (40%) did not employ any of laboratory notebook storage and retrieval system. The remaining respondents used one of four different S&R systems. All of these systems basically followed the same procedures in the assigning and storage of the notebooks. The wide variation among the systems occurred in the indexing and retrieval of the notebooks.

Procedures of Laboratory Notebook Systems

A. Notebook Assignment

The first step involved with a laboratory notebook storage and retrieval system—the assigning of a new notebook to the researcher—was similar in all of the surveyed food science libraries. The blank notebooks are numbered by the library before being issued to the researcher. A record of the notebook number, the researcher's name, and sometimes the date of issuance and general subject area is maintained in a bound log book or on individual cards arranged in numerical order by notebook number. In a few libraries, an additional card file arranged alphabetically by the assignee's name and containing a record of every notebook assigned to that individual is maintained. Among other uses, this additional file allows the library to recall the notebooks an employee has when he or she is ready to leave the company.

Although only one person supposedly uses a notebook, a notebook may be reassigned to cover continuations of similar work. This type of transaction is recorded in the card files or log book. When a notebook is completed, it is returned to the library for storage and future retrieval. In most cases, the notebooks are in numerical order since the most

TABLE 1: LAB NOTEBOOK STORAGE AND RETRIEVAL SYSTEMS

Index Systems Employed	Number of Libraries	Percentage
No Method	24	40
Informal	9	15
Accession Number	18	30
Additional Subject Access	8	13
Multiple Access Points	1	2
TOTAL	60	100%

recent information, which would be in the notebook with the highest number, would expected to be requested most frequently.

B. Notebook Storage

Since considerable time and money has been invested in the experimental work represented by the laboratory notebooks, all the libraries that were responsible for notebook storage stored the notebooks very securely in locked filing cabinets or in a vault. However, nine of the libraries stored their notebooks, not in hard copy, but on microfilm due to space limitations and security reasons. In this case, the original notebook is stored off site or returned to the appropriate researcher, while the microfilmed copy is retained by the library. Microfilm not only saves storage space and decreases the possibility of fire, but also eases duplication and distribution of the notebook to various scattered subdivisions within the organization. When used in combination with a retrieval terminal, such as the Kodak Oracle, notebook retrieval time can be improved.

C. Notebook Indexing and Retrieval

Several different approaches to indexing the notebook were used by the surveyed libraries. Nine of the 36 libraries who kept laboratory notebooks did not employ any systematic method of indexing and retrieval. The only means of access to these notebooks was from the researcher's memory or through references in progress and final project reports based on information in these notebooks.

The simplest indexing and retrieval procedure, which was used by 17 libraries, involved an accession number system. The card files used for assigning the blank notebooks were also used to retrieve the completed notebooks. One card file lists the notebooks in numerical order, stating the corresponding author, and another card file that was arranged alphabetically by author lists the corresponding notebook numbers. The majority of these card files were in the form of index cards. One library used coded microfilm, while another used IBM punch cards. With this indexing and retrieval arrangement, two access points are available; notebook number and author.

The major drawback to this system is the lack of direct subject access to the notebooks. Some of the libraries have tentatively planned to develop a subject index that would involve key words. Other libraries did not see a need for subject access because they had indirect subject access to the notebooks from the company research reports that summarized the notebooks. These reports, which are indexed by author, keywords, and sometimes project numbers frequently refer to the particular number of the notebook and/or its author.

A variant of this accessioning system involved the development of a project number index. One library provided this access point to their notebooks by maintaining three card files, each arranged according to laboratory notebook number, project number, and author. These cards also provided information such as inclusive dates covered in the notebooks, project title, or subject matter. The use of project number as an access point may overcome the lack of a subject index since notebooks covering the same project and having the same project number would probably contain information on similar subjects.

Eight libraries did devise a subject index in addition to the notebook number and author indexes. Five of these libraries maintained the subject index manually while the rest relied on computer generated subject indexes. In the manual mode, a general subject index was included in each notebook when it had been completed. These subject indexes are devised by the author of the notebook or by the library staff. In either case, access to the notebooks is available by means of general subject headings, as well as notebook number and author. However, there is no one master subject index to all of the notebooks. As a result, one has to locate the notebook first by author or notebook number and then search the individual subject indexes.

Two libraries which used a manual subject indexing procedure developed a simple master subject index to the notebooks. In one case, general subject cards, each with a numerical list of notebook numbers containing these subject headings, are made. The other library uses the contents pages of the individual notebooks and a cross index of notebook number, employee, period covered by the notebook, and general contents.

Three of the eight libraries maintaining subject indexes, generated computerized subject indexes. These computerized indexes employed either a KWIC (Key Word in Context) or a KWOC (Key Word Out of Context) indexing system. One library created a detailed KWOC index involving keywords, project numbers, and authors. The keywords, including names of projects, products, chemicals, and ingredients, for a series of 10-page blocks of each notebook are assigned by the scientist upon completion of the notebook. Then these terms for each block of 10 pages of a notebook are permuted to generate a computerized KWOC index. Thus, this indexing allows access almost to the exact page of the notebook.

One library used optical coincidence to obtain access to the notebooks by a combination of two or more subject headings. Optical coincidence, which is a coordinate card indexing system, is also known as the Termatrex system or Peek-a-Boo system.[7] Although this indexing and retrieval system provides short retrieval time and coordination of subject headings, it is impractical for collections larger than 10,000 items, due to the finite number of subject cards that can be feasibly employed.

One library used an indexing and retrieval system that offered many accessible points through the use of seven computerized indexes or logs. These logs included a notebook number log (a sequential list identifying who has each notebook); assignee log (alphanumeric list arranged by name of assignee and identifying all of the notebooks assigned to each assignee); department log (an alphabetical list of assignees arranged by department); and responsibility number log (an alphabetical list of assignees arranged by responsibility or shop order number). This library plans to develop a subject index, but for the present, subject access is available to the notebooks through the subject indexed laboratory reports.

General Drawbacks of All Systems

Some general drawbacks of notebook storage and retrieval systems were experienced by many of the libraries. One problem was the cooperation of the researchers in supplying the notebooks to the library upon completion. Many researchers do not find the time or do not want to take the time to participate in any notebook storage and retrieval system. Another drawback involved the degree of indexing being achieved in the present systems. A large number of libraries stated that they desired more detailed indexing of their notebooks, especially subject indexing.

Conclusion

There seems to be a total of four different laboratory notebook storage and retrieval systems at present employed by food science libraries. These systems include: 1) an informal, unorganized system; 2) an accessioning number system that involves author, notebook number, and sometimes project number; 3) an additional subject index in a manual or computerized form; 4) more complex computerized systems that allowed multiple access points. The most widely used system was the accession number system which allowed access by notebook number and notebook author.

With the continuing introduction of new technology in libraries, such as computerized microfilm retrieval systems, further research on the storage and retrieval systems used for laboratory notebooks, as well as other in-house publications, should be conducted.

REFERENCES

1. Hughson, Roy. How to keep laboratory notebooks. *Chemical Engineering.* 71(25): 182–186; 1964 December 7.
2. BASF Wyandotte Corporation. *Laboratory record keeping evaluation.* Mimeographed report. Wyandotte, MI: BASF Wyandotte Corporation; 1978 Summer.
3. Bailey, Martha. The laboratory notebook as a research and development record. *Special Libraries.* 63(4): 189–194; 1972 April.
4. Mendenhall, Donna. Indexing lab notebooks in a chemical R&D environment. *Special Libraries.* 69(7): 261–265; 1978 July.
5. Cibbarelli, Pamela [and others]. Libnotes: a laboratory notebook retrieval system. *In:* Brenner, E. H., ed. *Proceedings of the 41st annual meeting of ASIS: The Information Age in perspective.* New York: Knowledge Industry Pubs; 1978: p. 67–69.
6. Young, M.; [and others]. *Subject directory of special libraries and information centers.* Detroit, MI: Gale Research Co.; 1977: p. 285–292.
7. Khan, Paul; Rosen, Jocelyn. Systems for information retrieval in small laboratories. *Food Technology.* 56(6): 846–849; 1964 June.

NEW REFERENCE WORKS IN SCIENCE & TECHNOLOGY

Janice W. Bain, Editor

COAL

Bloch, Carolyn C. COAL INFORMATION SOURCES AND DATA BASES. *Park Ridge, N.J.: Noyes Data Corporation; 1980. 128 p. $24.00. ISBN 0-8155-0830-1.*

This directory comprises a comprehensive guide to federal, state, and international agencies, departments, offices and cooperating information sources, such as libraries and universities, that deal with coal data, whether it be legal or regulatory data, assistance programs, or data on research and technology. The directory supplies the address and a capsule description of each source, including its field of emphasis, services offered, and availability of publications. There is a detailed Table of Contents which precedes the text and serves as a guide to subject matter and an Index which provides a full listing of all the coal information and data sources. The directory will be of assistance to scientists, engineers, geologists, managers, librarians, and others directly involved with the use of coal data and information. *(CC)*

COMPUTERS

Sippl, Charles J.; Sippl, Roger J. COMPUTER DICTIONARY. *3d ed. Indianapolis: Howard W. Sams; 1980. 624 p. $12.95. ISBN 0-672-21652-3.*

This is described as a "browsing" dictionary intended for users of computers rather than for computer specialists. It is a tutorial book that does not try to be brief. Many definitions and explanations are long and are designed to be so. Users of the book can browse through the main and supplemental entries of an area to learn significant detail about the products, procedures, problems and applications involved. A number of photographs and diagrams are included. *(CC)*

Janice W. Bain is Librarian at the Transportation Research Board (National Research Council of the National Academy of Sciences), 2101 Constitution Avenue, Washington, DC 20418

ENERGY

Jacques Cattell Press, editor. ENERGY RESEARCH PROGRAMS. *New York: Bowker; 1980. 444 p. $75.00. ISBN 0-8352-1242-4.*

This publication marks the inauguration of a set of directories that will incorporate and expand the established format of *Industrial research laboratories of the United States*. *Energy research programs* is a multidisciplinary directory of energy-related programs, services, and industries. Included are 3,675 parent organizations having 5,900 research facilities. Coverage includes federal, state, provincial and local government organizations in the United States and Canada; academic research units in the United States and Canada; selected professional societies and agencies of the government of Mexico; expanded coverage of the petroleum and mining industries; engineering firms; and energy-related firms whose traditional laboratory research is minimal but whose contribution to the North American energy effort is substantial. The body of the directory is an alphabetical listing of principal, or parent, organizations. Corporate information is followed by a listing for the central research and development center, if any, and then by an alphabetical listing of all divisions and subsidiaries. Academic information lists colleges/divisions in alphabetical order with various departments and institutes within their respective colleges/divisions. Government units follow the same pattern with administrative units followed by departments/divisions in alphabetical order. Preceding each principal is an identification code. These identification codes are used in the Geographic, Personnel, and Subject indexes to refer the user to the proper entry. In general, the basic content of individual entries follows the same pattern established in *Industrial research laboratories of the United States*. Each entry ends with a statement of chief R&D activity. *(CC)*

ENERGY

SOLAR CENSUS: THE DIRECTORY FOR THE 80S. *Ann Arbor: aatec (sic) Publications; 1980. 484 p. $45.00. ISBN 0-937948-00-4.*

This biennial directory was compiled from questionnaires completed by solar energy professionals throughout the United States. Entries are divided into four major sections based on the primary activities designated by the respondents: Manufacturers; Design—Architecture and Engineering; Research and Development; and Education and Information. The entries are arranged alphabetically within each major section and assigned numerical entry codes to facilitate use of the four indexes—Alphabetical, Subject, Trade Name, and Geographical. *(CC)*

HEATING AND COOLING EQUIPMENT

Ecodyne Corporation. Cooling Products Division. WEATHER DATA HANDBOOK FOR HVAC AND COOLING EQUIPMENT DESIGN. *New York: McGraw-Hill; 1980. Various paging. $32.50. ISBN 0-07-018960-9.*

Reliable hourly weather information scanning a sufficient period to establish dependable frequency of occurrence levels supplies a base for reliable design calculations for heating, ventilating and air conditioning equipment. The data contained in this book represent detailed tabulations of wet bulb temperature frequencies for the summer months; tabulations in three frequency categories for winter and summer conditions; and tabulations of various weather parameters useful in estimating performance for wet/dry and natural draft cooling towers and other applications. In addition to the vast amount of new material included, this edition also contains material from the Fluor Products Company's *Evaluated weather data for cooling equipment design* (1958) and Addendum No. 1, 1964, which are no longer in print. The complete summaries from which this compilation was developed are available from the Cooling Products Division of the Ecodyne Corporation for use if a particular design problem should require more detailed or specific analysis *(CC)*

PSYCHIATRY

American Psychiatric Association. Subcommittee of the Joint Commission on Public Affairs. A PSYCHIATRIC GLOSSARY. *Boston: Little, Brown; 1980. 142 p: $9.95. ISBN 0-316-03656-0.*

This popular glossary has become a classic of its kind. First suggested by an organization of scientific writers, the glossary was and is intended chiefly for nonmedical personnel. However, students and practitioners in the health sciences have found it highly useful over the years, as have social workers, lawyers, and librarians. The fifth edition contains more than 1,000 commonly encountered psychiatric terms, and incorporates the revised nomenclature of the new APA *Diagnostic and statistical manual* (DSM-III). Certain categories of terms have been conveniently grouped in tables; e.g., "Psychological Tests," with appropriate cross references from the main body of the book. *(KH)*

Guttman, Samuel A. and others, editors. THE CONCORDANCE TO THE STANDARD EDITION OF THE COMPLETE PSYCHOLOGICAL WORKS OF SIGMUND FREUD. *Boston: G. K. Hall; 1980. 6 volumes. $525.00. ISBN 0-8161-8383-X.*

The computer-produced *Concordance* lists virtually every word written by Freud as translated in *The standard edition*, edited by James A. Strachey. The entries are presented alphabetically in a keyword-in-context (KWIC) format. Each quoted line of context includes the corresponding volume and page numbers in *The standard edition*, an abbreviated title of the article or essay from which the word comes, and the date when the work was first published. Thus researchers can trace terms and concepts chronologically. Included with *The Concordance* are two appendixes. The first ranks keywords by frequency; the term "dream" heads the list with 6113 entries. The second appendix is a pagination converter which permits the researcher to move from the quoted line in *The standard edition* to the original German text in Freud's *Gesammelte Werke*. This mammoth reference work is amazingly easy to use and will be a necessity in large university, medical, or psychiatric libraries. *(KH)*

Reviewers: Carmela Carbone (CC)
Karen Hall (KH)

SCI-TECH ONLINE

Ellen Nagle, Editor

Database News

Over 5 Million Chemical Substances Available for Substructure Search

Over 5 million substances reported in the world's scientific and technical literature since 1965 are now available for online searching through Chemical Abstracts Service's CAS ONLINE system. Substances within the file can be searched to identify those which share structural characteristics and which may therefore share properties or activities of interest. Answers retrieved in the search include structure diagrams, which can be displayed on the screen of a compatible graphics terminal or printed offline and forwarded to the searcher.

Information retrieved also includes the *Chemical Abstracts* index name and up to 10 synonyms (including common and trade names), the molecular formula and CAS Registry Number, a text descriptor that provides stereochemical information and, at the searcher's option, *Chemical Abstracts* abstract numbers for the 10 most recent references to the substance in the chemical literature. New substances reported in the scientific or technical literature are added to the file weekly. The file grows at the rate of about 6000 newly registered substances each week.

CAS ONLINE is on the CAS Chemical Registry System, a computer file of information on substances reported in journal articles, patents, technical reports, conference proceedings and dissertations since 1965. Detailed structural descriptions for the over 5 million unique substances are linked to names used to refer to these substances and to molecular formulas through an identifying Register Number.

CAS has set a low price for connect time with the system—$25 per terminal connect hour plus communication charges. A sample search costs $14, and a search of the full file is $77 in addition to connect time and telecommunications charges. Answers printed or displayed in a format which includes abstract numbers are $.25 per hit, while answers without abstract numbers are $.10 per hit. The system may be accessed through Telenet.

Ellen Nagle is Head, Reference Department, Health Sciences Library, Columbia University, 701 W. 168th St., New York, NY 10032.

CASSI Offered

SDC has announced the availability of the *Chemical Abstracts Service Source Index* (CASSI) online. CASSI provides bibliographic data, library holdings and information on publishers and document suppliers for journals or serials, monographs, and conference proceedings cited in the literature of the 19th and 20th century. Subject coverage includes chemistry, biology, engineering medicine, physics and all other sciences. Over 50,000 serial and non-serial publications are covered. Coverage is international and updates are quarterly.

Serial, monograph, and conference proceedings titles are derived from sources such as *Chemical Abstracts* since 1907, *Chemisches Zentralblatt* from 1830 to 1940, Beilstein's *Handbuch der Organischen Chemie* from its inception to 1965, 700 titles monitored by the BioSciences Information Service (BIOSIS), *Engineering Index*, the Original Article Tear Sheet service (OATS) of the Institute for Scientific Information, and the International Periodical Copy Service of University Microfilms. The connect hour rate for CASSI is $60 per hour; online prints are $.10 per citation; offline print charges vary according to format from $.10 to $.90 per citation.

Directory Databases Added

BRS is now offering 3 online directories and reference books, products of R. R. Bowker: *Books in Print, American Men and Women of Science*, and *Ulrich's International Periodicals Directory*.

The *Books in Print* database provides extensive bibliographic information on 640,000 titles that are either in print or declared out of print within the last two years. The database also includes up to 60,000 soon-to-be-published titles from *Forthcoming Books in Print*, as well as information from *Scientific and Technical Books in Print, Medical Books in Print*, and other Bowker bibliographies. Monthly updating of the database assures more current information than any of the print versions can provide.

American Men and Women of Science includes names, addresses, and detailed biographical information on more than 130,500 preeminent U. S. and Canadian scientists.

Ulrich's International Periodicals Directory (incorporating *Irregular Serials and Annuals*) provides information on 65,000 periodicals and 38,500 serials, annuals, continuations, conference proceedings, and other publications from around the world. Introductory prices for the 3 databases are at the royalty rate of $20 per hour for *Books in Print* and *Ulrich's*; $35 per hour for *American Men and Women of Science*.

Lockheed/DIALOG is offering *Biography Master Index* (BMI). Available as File 88, BMI is a master key to biographical information on nearly 2,000,000 persons who have distinguished themselves in hundreds of fields. It indexes approximately 375 biographical dictionaries and directories, including current works such as *Who's Who in America* as well as such retrospective sources as *Biographical Dictionary of*

American Science, 17th-19th Centuries. Each BMI record provides a person's name, the birth and death dates if available, and the titles of source books that provide complete biographical sketches on the person. The database corresponds to Gale Research Company's eight-volume publication, *Biography and Genealogy Master Index*, 2nd edition, and a similar microfiche product known as *Bio-Base*. The file will be updated on a periodic but unspecified basis. The price for searching BMI is $55 per connect hour, and $.15 for each full record printed offline.

Directory databases can be particularly valuable to sci-tech libraries. Many have highly specialized reference collections and do not purchase general reference tools. In addition, online directories give multiple access points enabling one to search on single words from book and journal titles, addresses of institutions, scientific specialties, etc.

ISI Databases Available

The Institute for Scientific Information has announced 3 new databases: *ISI/BIOMED, ISI/ISTP & B*, and *ISI/CompuMath*. All are accessible from the ISI Search Network via Telenet.

ISI/BIOMED is drawn from the *Science Citation Index* database and covers over 700,000 articles from more than 1200 journals worldwide in all biomedical disciplines from 1979 to date. The database is searchable by author or institution name, title words, language, document type, cited references, source journal, and year of publication. In addition, direct access is provided to "research front specialties" identified by ISI as "discrete, interacting, and sometimes overlapping areas of intense research activity and rapid advance." The rate for *ISI/BIOMED* is $1.70 per connect minute.

ISI/ISTP & B (Index to Scientific & Technical Proceedings & Books) is a multidisciplinary database to the proceedings and monographic literature. It includes more than 400,000 articles from over 10,000 proceedings, and in excess of 2000 books (including annual review series) in the sciences and technology. All books and proceedings are indexed at the chapter level. Coverage is from 1978 to the present with approximately 300 volumes added each month. The cost of searching is $1.70 per connect minute. A reduced rate of $.85 per connect minute is offered to current *ISTP* subscribers.

ISI/CompuMath covers over 200,000 articles from more than 290 journals and 40 books in mathematics, statistics, computer science, and operations research from 1976 to the present. Standard bibliographic fields as well as research front specialties are searchable. *ISI/CompuMath* is available at $.85 per connect minute. Access is restricted to subscribers to the *ISI/CompuMath* package of printed indexes.

BRS is offering access to *SCISEARCH*, ISI's online equivalent of *Science Citation Index*. Over 3800 leading journals from every discipline in science and technology are included; the time span covered is the current year plus one previous year. There are monthly updates of approximately 47,000 items. Royalty fees are $22 for *SCI* subscribers, and $90 for non-*SCI* subscribers.

MEDLINE on DIALOG

Lockheed/DIALOG is now offering the *MEDLINE* database from 1966 to the present available entirely online. *MEDLINE* created by the U.S. National Library of Medicine corresponds to three major printed indexes: *Index Medicus, Index to Dental Literature,* and *International Nursing Index.* Approximately 40% of the citations from 1975 forward contain author abstracts. DIALOG is offering rotated subject headings and an online thesaurus to aid in searching. The database is available as Files 154 (*MEDLINE* 1980 +), 153 (*MEDLINE* 1975-1979) and 152 (*MEDLINE* 1966-1974). Files are available for searching at $35 per connect hour and $.15 per full record with abstract or $.075 per record without abstract printed offline. SDI service is offered at $4.95 per month.

COMPENDEX Offered

COMPENDEX (*Computerized Engineering Index*) is now available through BRS; their version provides coverage of worldwide technical literature from 1976 to date. Broad subject categories include civil, environmental, geological, petroleum, mechanical, nuclear, aerospace, computer, electrical, chemical, and industrial engineering. The file contains approximately one million citations, and is updated monthly. *COMPENDEX* covers journals, conference proceedings, technical reports and monographs. The database is the online counterpart of *The Engineering Index.* Royalties are $25 per hour and $.10 per citation printed offline.

IRIS Offered by DIALOG

IRIS, the Instructional Resources Information System of the U.S. Environmental Protection Agency Information Dissemination Project at Ohio State University, has joined the DIALOG system as File 53. *IRIS* is a specialized file of abstracts of educational and instructional materials on water quality and water resource materials. The file includes journal articles, references to films, filmstrips, slides, brochures, pamphlets, and books. Its major emphasis is water quality and water resources, but it also includes other environment-related instructional materials. *IRIS* corresponds to the printed work *Water Quality Instructional Resources Information System.* *IRIS* is available at $35 per connect hour and $.10 per full record printed offline.

Search System News

DIALOG Information Services Established

Lockheed has announced the establishment of DIALOG Information Services, Inc. as a separate corporation which is a wholly-owned subsidiary of the Lockheed Corporation. Previously the DIALOG Information Retrieval Service was part of the Advance Systems Division of the

Lockheed Missiles and Space Company, Inc., also a subsidiary of the parent Lockheed Corporation:

DIALOG anticipates the continued support of Lockheed under this new arrangement, and promises "the flexibility necessary to be even more responsive" to its users' needs.

DIALOG Days

DIALOG has been offering "DIALOG Days" on the first Monday of every month, in service offices in major cities. Introductions to DIALOG are scheduled in the mornings; Customer Clinics in the afternoon assist searchers and provide consultations on problems searches.

BRS Collection Development Service Enhancement

BRS has added the capability of merging collection development reports of unrelated passwords. This enables subscribers to obtain single alphabetic and frequency lists. Combined collection development reports may be produced for libraries within a single system, libraries sharing subject or geographic resources, and for consortium development planning.

SDC Plans European Facility

System Development Corporation and Derwent Publications Ltd. have announced an agreement in principle to establish a European online information retrieval service as a joint-venture project. The objective of the new service is to address the requirements of the significant and rapidly growing European market for online information retrieval.

Computer operations at a European facility, using the ORBIT Information Retrieval System, and accessible via Euronet, are planned for installation by the end of this year. Initially, the facility will offer the Derwent databases. Once the service is established, additional databases will be added to address the specific needs and interests of the European community.

Price Changes

NLM Raises Online Charges Effective October 1, 1981, charges for NLM databases were increased as follows: *TOXLINE* and its backfiles are $35 per connect hour for prime time (10 am to 5 pm ET), $28 per connect hour in nonprime time; *CHEMLINE* is $59 per hour prime time, $52 per hour nonprime time; *MEDLINE* and all other databases are $22 per connect hour for prime time, and $15 per hour for nonprime time. These increases include royalty charges of $13 for the *TOXLINE* files and $37.64 for *CHEMLINE*.

Following suit, BRS has increased the connect hour rate on *MEDLARS* and the *Health* file to $15 per hour. Adding the telecommunications charge of $7 per hour, the BRS rate conforms to the NLM charge of $22 per hour.

ASFA Price Increase Effective October 1, 1981, DIALOG raised the price for searching *Aquatic Sciences and Fisheries,* File 44, to $62 per connect hour. The print rate remains at $.20 per full record. The price increase was necessitated by an increase in royalty charges by the database supplier.

BIOSIS Offline Print Reductions SDC has announced variable rates for different print options on its 3 BIOSIS files. Full or tailored formats now cost $.20 per citation; standard print and print trial citations are $.10 each. A new format "print issue" which lists accession number, title, and source fields costs $.05 per citation. Print issue enables a requestor to go to the printed index to get additional information. These reductions reflect a significant change from the former rate of $.25 per citation.

CRIS/USDA Prime Reduced DIALOG has reduced the rate for searching the U.S. Department of Agriculture's *Current Research Information System (CRIS).* Connect hour charges are now $35 rather than $40. Users with subscription contracts may have reductions of up to $20 per connect hour, depending on level of usage.

AGRICOLA Price Increased Effective May 1, 1981, the price of *AGRICOLA* has been increased by DIALOG to $30 per connect hour and $.10 per offline print. DIALOG attributes the increase to the extra programming efforts necessitated by the data presented to them.

METADEX Print Charges Raised Effective August 1, DIALOG increased the charges for online and offline printing in *METADEX,* File 32. The new rates are $.10 per full record online; $.15 for full record offline.

For Product Safety Concerns and Information please contact our EU
representative GPSR@taylorandfrancis.com
Taylor & Francis Verlag GmbH, Kaufingerstraße 24, 80331 München, Germany

www.ingramcontent.com/pod-product-compliance
Lightning Source LLC
Chambersburg PA
CBHW052135300426
44116CB00010B/1913